ECONOMICS AFTER NEOLIBERAL- ISM

This publication was made possible by a generous grant from
THE WILLIAM AND FLORA HEWLETT FOUNDATION

Editors-in-Chief Deborah Chasman & Joshua Cohen

Executive Editor Chloe Fox

Managing Editor and Arts Editor Adam McGee

Senior Editor Matt Lord

Engagement Editor Rosie Gillies

Contributing Editors Junot Díaz, Adom Getachew, Walter Johnson, Robin D.G. Kelley, Lenore Palladino

Contributing Arts Editors Ed Pavlić & Evie Shockley

Editorial Assistant Stijn P. Talloen

Publisher Louisa Daniels Kearney

Marketing and Development Manager Dan Manchon

Finance Manager Anthony DeMusis III

Distributor The MIT Press, Cambridge, Massachusetts, and London, England

Printer Sheridan PA

Board of Advisors Derek Schrier (chairman), Archon Fung, Deborah Fung, Alexandra Robert Gordon, Richard M. Locke, Jeff Mayersohn, Jennifer Moses, Scott Nielsen, Robert Pollin, Rob Reich, Hiram Samel, Kim Malone Scott

Interior Graphic Design Zak Jensen & Alex Camlin

Cover Design Alex Camlin

Economics After Neoliberalism is *Boston Review* Forum 11 (44.3)

To become a member, visit:
bostonreview.net/membership/

For questions about donations and major gifts,
contact: Dan Manchon, dan@bostonreview.net

For questions about memberships, call 877-406-2443
or email Customer_Service@bostonreview.info.

Boston Review
PO Box 425786, Cambridge, MA 02142
617-324-1360

ISSN: 0734-2306 / ISBN: 978-1-946511-45-4

CONTENTS

ESSAYS

EDITOR'S NOTE
Joshua Cohen

NEAR THE END of *Capitalism and Freedom* (1962), Milton Friedman states the central thesis of his influential book: "Equality comes sharply into conflict with freedom; one must choose. One cannot be both an egalitarian . . . and a liberal." What Friedman calls "liberalism" is the market fundamentalism that is now commonly called "neoliberalism."

Friedman's argument, radical in 1962, became the country's guiding public philosophy with Ronald Reagan's election in 1980. Its power as public philosophy owed less to the compelling force of its economic analysis than to its success in recruiting the value of liberty—our "equal right to freedom"—to its cause. Recruiting liberty, while dismissing equality and subordinating the civic liberty associated with democracy.

We are now living with the consequences of this experiment: a socially pathological concentration of income and wealth; a decades-long assault on the capacity of public institutions to address our most fundamental problems, including climate catastrophe; a collapse of working-class communities, black, brown, and white; a blame-the-victim philosophy of "personal responsibility"; and an assault on the commitments to civic equality, public reason, and shared responsibility that are essential to a flourishing democracy.

Some people—including newly self-styled "nationalist conservatives"—blame the "left" for all this damage. On Earth, things look different. We live in a world made by neoliberalism, with its hostility to equality and democracy. It is time to stop.

This issue of *Boston Review*—published with generous support from the Hewlett Foundation—suggests new directions. It explores the destructive impact of shareholder primacy, the role of law in consolidating unequal power, and the importance of public communication of economic ideas in democracy. Its core is the debate generated by three influential economists—Suresh Naidu, Dani Rodrik, and Gabriel Zucman—who argue that economics must break decisively from the anti-egalitarian, antidemocratic market fundamentalism of the neoliberal revolution and embrace an economics of "inclusive prosperity." Their essay, the project they have launched, and the rich debate they have provoked may be the start of something new and important—we are calling it *Economics After Neoliberalism*.

FORUM

ECONOMICS AFTER NEOLIBERAL- ISM

Suresh Naidu, Dani Rodrik,
& Gabriel Zucman

We live in an age of astonishing inequality. Income and wealth disparities in the United States have risen to heights not seen since the Gilded Age and are among the highest in the developed world. Median wages for U.S. workers have stagnated for nearly fifty years. Fewer and fewer younger Americans can expect to do better than their parents. Racial disparities in wealth and well-being remain stubbornly persistent. In 2017 life expectancy in the United States declined for the third year in a row, and the allocation of healthcare looks both inefficient and unfair. Advances in automation and digitization threaten greater labor market disruptions in the years ahead. Climate change–fueled disasters increasingly disrupt everyday life.

We believe that these are solvable problems—at the very least, that we can make serious headway on them. But addressing them will require a broad public discussion of new policy ideas. Social scientists have a responsibility to be part of this discussion. And economists have an indispensable role to play. Indeed, they have already started to play it. Economics is in a state of creative ferment that is often invisible to outsiders. While the sociology of the profession—career incentives, norms, socialization patterns—often militates against engagement with the policy world, a sense of public responsibility is bringing people into the fray.

The tools of economics are critical to developing a policy framework for what we call "inclusive prosperity." While prosperity is the traditional concern of economists, the modifier "inclusive" demands both that we consider the whole distribution of outcomes, not simply the average (the "middle class"), and that we consider human prosperity broadly, including nonpecuniary sources of well-being, from health to climate change to political rights. To improve the quality of public discussion around inclusive prosperity, we have organized a group of economists—the Economics for Inclusive Prosperity (EfIP) network—to make policy recommendations across a range of topics, including labor markets, international trade, and finance. The purpose of this nascent effort is not simply to offer a list of prescriptions for different policy domains, but to provide an overall vision for economic policy that stands as an alternative to the market fundamentalism that is often—and wrongly—identified with economics.

We personally saw the power of this identification in early 2018, when the three of us attended a workshop on "new thinking beyond neoliberalism." The participants—historians, political scientists, sociologists, legal scholars, and economists—agreed that the prevailing neoliberal policy framework had failed society, resulting in monumental and growing inequality. All of us were horrified by the illiberal, nativist turn in our politics, fueled in part by these chasms. There was consensus around the need for a genuine alternative—a set of policies that were both effective and inclusive, responding to legitimate grievances without sowing deeper societal divisions.

Although we fully embraced these aims, we found ourselves on the defensive. In the eyes of many, the turn toward neoliberalism is closely associated with economic ideas. Leading economists such as Friedrich Hayek and Milton Friedman were among the founders of the Mont Pelerin Society, the influential group of intellectuals whose advocacy of markets and hostility to government intervention proved highly effective in reshaping the policy landscape after 1980. Deregulation, financialization, dismantling of the welfare state, deinstitutionalization of labor markets, reduction in corporate and progressive taxation, and the pursuit of hyper-globalization—the culprits behind rising inequalities—all seem to be rooted in conventional economic doctrines. The discipline's focus on markets and incentives, methodological individualism, and mathematical formalism stand in the way of meaningful, large-scale reform. In short, neoliberalism appears to be just another name for economics.

Consequently, many people view the discipline with outright hostility. They believe the teaching and practice of economics has to be fundamentally reformed for the discipline to become a constructive force. There are, indeed, legitimate reasons for discontent with the way economics is often practiced and taught. Conservative foundations and think tanks have monopolized the banner of economics in policy circles, pushing the view that there is a steep efficiency–equality trade-off and assigning priority to economic growth. Students often leave their introductory economics courses thinking that "markets always work." Conservatives tend to deploy "economics" as a justification for preferred policies, while liberals are seen as insensitive to the requirements for prosperity.

Our response is fundamentally different. Many of the dominant policy ideas of the last few decades are supported neither by sound economics nor by good evidence. Neoliberalism—or market fundamentalism, market fetishism, etc.—is not the consistent application of modern economics, but its primitive, simplistic perversion. And contemporary economics is rife with new ideas for creating a more inclusive society. But it is up to economists to convince our audience about the merits of these claims, which is why we have embarked on this project. Below, we have outlined a set of policy briefs (full versions are available online) that we hope will stimulate and accelerate economists' engagement with creative ideas for inclusive prosperity.

BEFORE WE GET to policy proposals, however, we must first address the issue of how to persuade non-economists that economics is part of the solution. To be sure, many economists' habits, especially when it comes to how they engage in public debates, are to blame for the misunderstanding of what economics is and what economists do.

Naidu, Rodrik, & Zucman

Economists study markets (among other things), and we naturally feel a certain pride in explaining the way markets operate. When markets work well, they do a good job of aggregating information and allocating scarce resources. The principle of comparative advantage, which lies behind the case for free trade, is one of the profession's crown jewels—both because it explains important aspects of the international economy and because it is, on its face, so counterintuitive. Similarly, economists believe in the power of incentives; we have evidence that people respond to incentives, and we have seen too many well-meaning programs fail because they did not pay adequate attention to the creative ways in which people behave to realize their own goals.

Yet too many economists believe their quantitative tools and theoretical lenses are the only ones that count as "scientific," leading them to dismiss disciplines that rely more on qualitative analysis and verbal theorizing. Many economists feel they need to take the side of markets because no one else will and because doing otherwise might "provide ammunition to barbarians" (i.e., self-interested pressure groups and rent-seekers). And even when some economists recognize market failures, they worry government action will make things worse and sweep many of the discipline's caveats under the rug. Economists thus get labeled as cheerleaders for free markets and hyper-globalization.

Economists also often get overly enamored with models that focus on a narrow set of issues and identify first-best solutions in the circumscribed domain, at the expense of potential complications and adverse implications elsewhere. A growth economist, for example, will analyze policies that enhance technology and innovation without worrying about labor market consequences. A trade economist will recommend reducing tariffs and assume that devising compensatory mechanisms for people who lose their jobs is somebody else's responsibility. And a finance economist will design regulations to make banks safe, without considering how these may interact with macroeconomic cycles. Many policy failures—the excesses of deregulation, hyper-globalization, tax cuts, fiscal austerity—reflect such first-best reasoning. To be useful, economists have to evaluate policies in the totality of the context in which they will be implemented and consider the robustness of policies to many possible institutional configurations and political contingencies.

But these bad habits aside, contemporary economics is hardly a paean to markets and selfishness. The typical course in microeconomics spends more time on market failures and how to fix them than on the magic of competitive markets. The typical macroeconomics course focuses on how governments can solve problems of unemployment, inflation, and instability rather than on the "classical" model where the economy is self-adjusting. The typical finance course revolves around financial crises, excessive risk-taking, and other malfunctions of financial systems. In fact, the "competitive equilibrium model" in which free markets are maximally efficient—even if they are not good for fair distribution—is the dominant framework only in introductory economics courses. Thoughtful economists (of which there are many) quickly move away from it.

Economics is still somewhat insular within the social sciences because of its methodological individualism, model-based abstraction, and mathematical and statistical formalism. But in recent decades, economists have reached out to other disciplines, incorporating many of their insights. Economic history is experiencing a revival, behavioral economics has put *homo economicus* on the defensive, and the study of culture has become mainstream. At the center of the discipline, distributional considerations are making a comeback. And economists have been playing an important role in studying the growing concentration of wealth, the costs of climate change, the concentration of important markets, the stagnation of income for the working class, and the changing patterns in social mobility.

Economists still have a strong bias toward market-based policy solutions, and their policy prescriptions tend to be narrowly focused on addressing precise market failures. For example, to address global warming, economists are likely to support putting a steep price on carbon. But the science of economics has never produced predetermined policy conclusions. In fact, all predictions and conclusions in economics are contingent: if x and y conditions hold, then z outcomes follow. The answer to almost any question in economics is "it depends," followed by an exegesis on what it depends on and why. Back in 1975, economist Carlos F. Diaz-Alejandro wrote, "by now any bright graduate student, by choosing his assumptions . . . carefully, can produce a consistent model yielding just about any policy recommendation he favored at the start." Economics has become even richer in the intervening four decades. We might say, only slightly facetiously, that today the graduate student need not even be that bright!

Moreover, economics research has become significantly more applied and empirical since the 1990s. The share of academic publications that use data and carry out empirical analysis has increased substantially in all subfields and currently exceeds 60 percent in labor economics, development economics, international economics, public finance, and macroeconomics. This is important because systematic empirical evidence is a disciplining device against ideological policy prescriptions. The recent empirical bent makes it more difficult to idolize markets because it makes it more difficult to ignore inconvenient facts. Recent empirical findings, for example, show that international trade produces large adverse effects on some local communities; minimum wages do not reduce employment; and financial liberalization produces crises rather than faster economic growth.

Economics does have its universals, of course, such as market-based incentives, clear property rights, contract enforcement, macroeconomic stability, and prudential regulation. These higher-order principles are generally presumed to be conducive to superior economic performance. But these principles are compatible with an almost infinite variety of institutional arrangements with each arrangement producing a different distributional outcome and a different contribution to overall prosperity. The recipe thus calls for comparative institutional analysis of economic performance—not glib "markets work" slogans. The abstraction with which economists perceive complex bundles of institutions also gives practitioners tools to help design large-scale alternatives—from precision tweaks to the tax code to full-blown visions of post-capitalist societies.

Consider even the simplest economic setting of a perfectly competitive market economy. When an economist draws a supply-and-demand diagram on the black board, she may not list all the institutional prerequisites that lie behind the two curves. Firms have property rights over their assets and can enforce their contracts with suppliers. They have access to credit, can rely on public infrastructure such as transportation and power, and are protected from thieves and bandits. Their employees accept the terms of employment and show up at work each day. Consumers have all the information they need to make reasonable choices. They are reasonably confident that firms do not cheat them. There is a stable unit of value and means of exchange for buying and selling goods.

Clearly markets rely on a wide range of institutions; they are "embedded" in institutions, as Karl Polanyi would say. But how should those institutions be designed? Take property rights as an example. The Coase theorem suggests it does not matter for efficiency how property rights are allocated as long as transaction costs are zero. But the caveat does a lot of work here: transaction costs matter greatly. So, we must make choices. Should a job belong to a company, a worker, or a combination? Perhaps the company itself should be owned by a third party—a local government entity, say—and simply ensure incentive compatibility for managers and workers. That might sound crazy to most Americans, but China has eked unprecedented rates of economic growth out of such a property-rights regime. Perhaps employers should have property rights (for a fixed period) only over new assets they create, with existing assets distributed among other claimants. That too sounds crazy, unless we realize that is exactly what the patent system does, giving innovators temporary ownership over new "intellectual property." Perhaps the government, on behalf of the general public, should retain part ownership of new technologies since so much of innovation relies on public infrastructure (public R&D and subsidies, higher education, the legal regime, etc.). The choices that need to be made must consider distributional concerns and depend both on our ultimate objectives and the potential fit with local context.

As we grapple with new realities created by digitization, demographics, and their impacts on labor markets, such questions about the allocation of property rights among different claimants become crucial. Economics does not necessarily have definite answers here. Nor does it provide the appropriate distributional weights (how to weigh the returns to workers, employers, and the government, and what procedural and deontological constraints should be respected). But it does supply the tools needed to lay out the trade-offs, thus contributing to a more informed democratic debate.

The same kind of institutional indeterminacy pervades all other policy domains. Which labor market institutions minimize job insecurity without jeopardizing employment creation? How do we best provide social protection without blunting economic incentives? What kind of financial regulations ensure financial stability without blocking financial innovation? What kind of monetary and fiscal rules are best for an open economy? Economics does not provide a fixed answer to these questions. Instead, it highlights the potential consequences of different arrangements.

There exists today a considerable variety of institutional arrangements. Welfare and labor-market arrangements, for example, differ greatly across the developed world, and the United States can learn a lot from experiments elsewhere. But plausible institutional diversity is not limited to existing practices. We can— and will need to—develop new institutions. Nothing in laissez-faire guarantees that growth will be equitable or globalization sustainable. We need to design policies and institutions that make inclusive prosperity possible and globalization sustainable—politically and economically. With a powerful theoretical machinery that allows them to think in abstract terms about such matters, economists are crucial to the task.

ALL OF THE PARTICIPANTS in our inclusive prosperity project are tenured academic economists, working in broadly mainstream subfields. Some have worked in government; most have not. Some have engaged in writing broadly for a nonacademic audience; most have not. They are researchers who believe sound scholarship is indispensable to inclusive prosperity. They are economists of the real world, who understand that we live in a second-best world rife with market imperfections and in which power matters enormously in shaping market outcomes.

In such a world, the competitive model is rarely the right benchmark for understanding problems and suggesting solutions. We must instead search for alternative models, which requires an empirical orientation, an experimental mind-set, and a good dose of humility to recognize the limits of our knowledge.

The policy proposals put forth reflect economic reasoning and contemporary evidence on a variety of market failures, from international trade to insurance to capital and labor markets. Throughout the proposals is the sense that economies are operating well inside the justice-efficiency frontier, and that there are numerous policy "free lunches" that could push us towards an economy that is morally better without sacrificing (and, indeed, possibly enhancing) prosperity. Taking contemporary economics seriously is consistent with recommending fairly dramatic structural changes in U.S. economic life.

Many of the proposals involve efficiency-and-equality enhancing interventions in markets well known to be rife with failure, such as labor markets, credit markets, insurance markets, and markets for innovation. While the theoretical basis for market failures in these domains has been apparent for some time, the empirical importance of the various failures has been made apparent only recently.

For example, in the minimum wage debate, few would claim that it is an effective tool for intervening in labor markets with wages above a certain level. Other labor market institutions are needed to take advantage of free lunches created by monopsony and other labor market failures in the segment of the labor market where most workers find themselves. Arindrajit Dube proposes a system of wage boards, similar to the Australian system, where either administrators or tripartite boards negotiate wages at the industry-occupation-region level, thus setting minimum wages throughout the distribution. He finds that wage inequality would significantly fall as a result. Suresh Naidu discusses the more traditional U.S. labor movement, and how mechanism design, experiments, and behavioral economics can be mobilized to ease the pervasive collective action problem facing unions.

In the domain of capital markets, both Anat Admati and Atif Mian stress the systemic risk produced by the current system. Mian discusses the role that inequality, together with capital flows from oil-rich countries and Asia, has played in generating a "glut" of U.S. savings, pushing down the real interest rate and increasing systemic risk. He shows how inequality generates instability in financial markets, but also how private macro-prudential contracting is thwarted because of externalities that contractors are not paying attention to and because of specific tax and regulatory structures (e.g., Basel III risk weighting). Exploring the banking sector, Admati shows how banks, uniquely among financial institutions, are overexposed to debt, making them more vulnerable to bankruptcy and a threat to stability. Both authors point to a variety of good regulatory options, with Mian emphasizing credit contract repayments that are contingent on the aggregate state of the economy, and Admati favoring capital requirements and tax reforms that make debt look less attractive.

Some of the proposals speak directly to how the size of the government can be increased in a sustainable and prosperity-enhancing way. Gabriel Zucman's proposal shows an ingeniously simple path out of international tax competition, where countries no longer have to bid for multinational investment by slashing corporate taxes. Zucman proposes taxing multinationals by allocating their global profits proportionally to where they make their sales. While companies can easily relocate profits or production to low-tax jurisdictions, sales are much harder to manipulate. His reform would thus make it possible to tax the winners of globalization, which seems like a necessary condition for globalization to be sustainable.

Sandra Black and Jesse Rothstein use the best modern economics to provide a contemporary restatement of an old idea: government should provide public goods and social insurance. Social insurance mitigates the widespread and well-known failures in insurance markets, in the form of unemployment insurance, social security, and health insurance. And education requires government provision because children are generally in school before the peak income of their parents and because parents cannot borrow against the earnings of their children. The benefits of education are also in the far future and are associated with externalities in crime, citizenship, and innovation. All this militates in favor of government provision of education and social insurance.

Anton Korinek takes up the increasingly important question of how new technologies affect labor markets and the distribution of income. The direction of technological change is not exogenous, he argues, and it depends on the incentives set both by markets and by governments. In particular, innovators may overestimate the social cost of labor, investing too much in technologies that replace labor. Governments routinely intervene in the process of innovation—to encourage green technologies, for example. Korinek proposes that they similarly steer technology in the direction of innovations that have desirable distributive properties. They could, for example, promote AI systems that complement and augment the cognitive abilities of workers—along with mechanisms that ensure workers retain a substantial part of the surplus generated. Korinek also discusses how inelastic, complementary factors such as land or specialized skills might be taxed in response to technological change, and how the value of monopolies granted by the patent system is intrinsically inegalitarian since it transfers income from consumers to owners of firms.

Dani Rodrik's proposal is distinctive in that it gives an explicitly prosocial justification for restrictions on trade, not trying to clothe the protectionism in terms of ameliorating some other externality or market failure. He shows that trade agreements ought to include clauses that prevent competition on "unjust" margins, and his "social safeguards" would give countries a claim, justified by broad social support, that a restriction on trade is necessary to maintain the domestic social contract. This proposal is indicative of the commitments of many of the members of EfIP: a willingness to subordinate textbook economic efficiency to other values such as democratic rule and egalitarian relationships among citizens. These proposals take Polanyi's words to heart: to work well, crucial markets (including markets for labor, land, and capital) must be embedded in nonmarket institutions, and the "rules of the game" must be supplied by government.

Finally, some of the proposals propose fixing nonmarket institutions with ideas from economics. Democratic political economy—where people's influence on policy is roughly equal and political preferences are arrived at through open, well-informed public debate—must be considered for any policy proposals in 2019. Too many policy ideas break on the rock of government capture by special interests or systematically distorted presentations in the media. Ethan Kaplan draws on a few decades of empirical political economy to suggest policies that could drastically alter the balance of political influence in the United States. His proposal exemplifies the strengths of empirical political economy as practiced in economics departments. The evidence cited is carefully identified from naturally occurring variation and suggests a number of policies that could equalize political representation and increase turnout. Some of these suggestions highlight margins more likely to be thought of by an economist than a political scientist: for example, the increased influence of money when media coverage of politics is low suggests that politicians, behaving somewhat rationally, trade off responsiveness across pecuniary and popular constituencies.

These proposals—which, again, are available on EfIP's website—share the theme of how power asymmetries shape our contemporary economy. Many economists dismiss the role of power because they think it cannot be studied rigorously or belongs outside economics. As Naidu puts it in his essay, "under conditions of perfect competition and information, there is no scope for power." But asymmetries between different groups abound: who has the upper hand in bargaining for wages and employment; who has market power and who gets to compete; who can move across borders and who is stuck at home; who can evade taxation and who cannot; who gets to set the agenda of trade agreements and who is excluded; who can vote and who is disenfranchised. Some of these asymmetries are traditional political imbalances; others are power imbalances that naturally occur in the market due to informational asymmetries or barriers to entry.

Policies that counter such asymmetries make sense not only from a distributional standpoint but also for improving aggregate economic performance. The EfIP project tackles these asymmetries frontally and suggest ways of rebalancing power for economic ends. Unions and wage boards can rein monopsony power in labor markets (Naidu and Dube); putting sand in the wheels of financial globalization can enhance the fiscal capacity of the state (Zucman); regulating private finance can prevent crises (Admati and Mian); giving labor a greater say in trade agreements can improve the design of trade agreements (Rodrik); and restricting campaign contributions and making it easier for poorer people to vote can increase the accountability of the political system (Kaplan).

But while these ideas range over a wide swathe of policy domains—social policy, taxation, labor markets, financial regulation, trade agreements, technology, and electoral rules—their coverage is certainly not exhaustive. Many important policy areas remain untouched. We offer them as evidence that economics produces relevant and imaginative policy ideas and an encouragement to other economists to contribute in the same vein. They are proof of concept for the claim that economics can help build a society that is both fairer and does more to live up to its productive potential—that economics can serve inclusive prosperity.

FORUM RESPONSES

ECONOMICS IS THE MATERIALITY
OF MORAL CHOICE
Corey Robin

FOR NON-ECONOMISTS on the left, "Economics After Neoliberalism" is a welcome arrival. Having long been scolded or silenced by neoliberals with a dismissive "You just don't understand how markets work," outsiders like me can only celebrate the assistance that Naidu, Rodrik, and Zucman provide—from deep within the inner sanctum no less. It almost feels like our Marshall McLuhan moment.

I wonder if Naidu, Rodrik, and Zucman are selling themselves short, however. To hear them tell it, what has made neoliberalism so attractive and commanding as a politics is the borrowed authority of economics. Neoliberals sold their policies as the simple implementation of economic knowledge, so much so that neoliberalism "now appears to be just another name for economics." Given that conflation, Naidu, Rodrik, and Zucman see their task as, first, debunking the notion that neoliberalism rests on "sound economics," and, second, offering progressive policy alternatives that incorporate values—such as "fairness," "equality," and "inclusive prosperity"—that neoliberals and some economists consider external to the discipline. The point is to marshal the technical knowledge of the profession on behalf of new values, policies, and institutions.

Since Friedrich Hayek is one of the avatars of the neoliberal turn, it is worth revisiting how he envisioned the task of the neoliberal economist, especially because he was operating in a comparable moment for the right—that is, when social democracy rather than neoliberalism seemed coterminous with economics. Because Hayek's conception of the economist's task is different from how Naidu, Rodrik, and Zucman conceive of that task, it may offer a useful perspective on the best way forward.

By the mid-1930s, Hayek believed his beleaguered band of brothers—including Ludwig von Mises and Lionel Robbins—had won the economic debate of socialism versus capitalism. They had demonstrated—not just once (in Red Vienna after World War I), but twice (in 1930s Britain, as well)—that it was not possible for socialist planners to gather and process the necessary information to anticipate and provide for the needs of a modern society without private property, the price mechanism, and other market institutions.

But that victory, Hayek came to realize, was pyrrhic. For the questions at stake were not just technical; they were moral and political. As he put it in a pioneering article from 1939, "Many planners would be willing to put up with a considerable decrease of efficiency if at that price greater distributive justice could be achieved." The crucial question, he said, was "one of ideals other than merely material welfare." Far from resting neoliberalism on the authority of the natural sciences or mathematics (forms of inquiry Hayek and Mises sought to distance their work from) or on the technical knowledge of economists (as Naidu, Rodrik, and Zucman claim), Hayek recognized that the argument for capitalism had to be won on moral and political grounds through the political arts of persuasion.

Here's where things get interesting. Though Hayek abandoned formal economics for social theory after the 1930s, his social theory remained dedicated to elaborating what he saw as the essential problem of economics: how to allocate finite resources between different purposes when society cannot agree on its basic ends. With its emphasis on the irreconcilability of our moral ends—the fact that members of a modern society do not and cannot agree on a scale of values—Hayek's point was fundamentally political, the sort of insight that has agitated everyone from Thomas Hobbes to John Rawls and Jürgen Habermas. Hayek was unique, however, in arguing that the political point was best addressed—indeed, could only be addressed—in the realm of the economic. No other discourse—not moral philosophy, political theory, psychology, or theology—understood so well that our ultimate moral values and political purposes get expressed and revealed only under conditions of radical economic constraint—when one is forced to assign a limited set of resources to ends that favor different sectors of society.

Morals are not really morals if they are not material, Hayek believed. Outside the constraining circumstance of the economy, our moral claims are so much wind. Inside the economy, they assume force and depth, achieving a revelatory clarity and profundity. "The sphere where material circumstances force a choice upon us," Hayek wrote in *The Road to Serfdom* (1944), "is the air in which alone moral

Robin

sense grows and in which moral values are daily re-created." For this reason, Hayek concluded that "economic life is not a sector of human life which can be separated from" other spheres of life, including our moral life. Economic life "is the administration of the means for all our different ends. Whoever takes charge of these means must determine which ends shall be served, which values are to be rated higher and which lower—in short, what men should believe and strive for."

The intrinsic links between moral and economic life, as well as the intractability of moral conflict, were the kernels of insight that animated Hayek's most far-reaching writing against socialism. The socialist presumes an agreement on ultimate ends: the putatively shared understanding of principles such as justice or equality is supposed to make it possible for state planners to conceive of their task as technical, as the neutral application of an agreed-upon rule. But no such agreement exists, Hayek insisted, and if it is presumed to exist, nothing will reveal its nonexistence more quickly than the attempt to implement it in practice.

Now we come back to Naidu, Rodrik, and Zucman. What strikes me about their text is its boldness at the level of policy, but its modesty at the level of public philosophy. That may be deliberate. But if it is, it may reinforce the very neoliberalism that it is meant to contest, insofar as it presumes that what the economist has to offer is neutral or technical authority on behalf of assumed moral ends such as justice or equality or inclusiveness—values for which we do not have shared definitions. That was precisely the claim that Hayek sought to refute, and I am not sure if Naidu, Rodrik, and Zucman have a response. Conversely, I fear that if they continue the course they have set on, showing that alternative policies are technically feasible, they may find themselves foundering on the same shoals as Hayek did before his turn to social theory: invoking economic knowledge when the field of play is in fact moral and political.

Hayek translated moral and political problems into an economic idiom. What we need now, I would argue, is a way to uninstall or reverse that translation. Karl Marx attempted just such a project, but his answers were elusive. In a fascinating but little-known 1927 essay, "On Freedom," Karl Polanyi also attempted such a project, giving us a stylized rendition of what it would mean for a political collective, rather than a firm or a consumer, to make an economic decision—not in the marketplace, where price helps determine our decisions, but in a deliberative assembly, where other considerations are at play. One part of the assembly, representing the interests of the collective, will want to make an investment in a long-term good; healthcare was the example Polanyi chose. Another part of the assembly, representing the workers who would have to make the specific sacrifices for that good, resists that decision. What to do? Argue it out, says Polanyi. Whatever is the final decision, it will be "a direct, internal choice, for here ideals within people are confronted with their costs; here everyone has to decide what his ideals are worth to him."

Notice that Polanyi does not presume any agreement about moral and political ends, as Hayek claimed socialists must. Notice how insistent he is that decisions about production must confront the question of costs. Like Hayek, Polanyi is attuned to the materiality of moral choice, only he believes the question of costs

Robin

and constraints is best mediated through moral and political arguments in the public square.

Hayek persuaded generations of elites that it is only the individual in the market who can engage in such a process. In a modern society, the combination of informational challenges, on the one hand, and the intractability of moral conflict, on the other, was seen as too great to make decisions about economic life through public deliberation. Like the generation of leftists from the early twentieth century, Naidu, Rodrik, and Zucman have an opportunity to reopen this question not just for elites (Hayek's preferred audience) but for society as a whole: to ask whether it should be a political collective rather than the market that makes decisions about social value.

Polanyi thought that nothing less than human freedom was at stake in how we answer that question. Hayek, coming from the opposite end of the spectrum, did as well. Maybe it is time for us to ask why and start talking about it again.

ECONOMICS AFTER PARTISANSHIP

Oren Cass

A DEFINING FEATURE of Naidu, Rodrik, and Zucman's essay is its close alignment with the Democratic Party. Indeed, its initial set of policy proposals would fit comfortably within the platforms of many candidates seeking the party's presidential nomination.

This congruence is not an indictment per se. Perhaps one of the nation's political parties did stumble upon just the right economic outlook despite a fatally flawed neoliberalism dominating academic and popular economic thinking. But two other explanations seem more plausible. First, that their essay restates economic views widely held during the period they want to transcend. And second, that the changes proposed are less economic than political in nature and the values chosen are ones that reinforce a particular set of political preferences.

On the first issue, the essay equates "market fundamentalism, market fetishism, etc." with neoliberalism and rejects it in favor of a model more sensitive to market failure. But market fetishism does not provide the basis for U.S. economics or public policy. In the academic realm, the authors themselves acknowledge that "contemporary economics is hardly a paean to markets and selfishness." And in the policy realm, it is not as if a bunch of market fundamentalists have actually cut back government provisions. Across Democratic and Republican congresses and presidencies, the United States has undertaken massive expansions of its safety net, entitlement programs, and public education systems; reregulation of the financial sector; and tightening of environmental standards, coupled with investments in clean energy.

Certainly, some economists and policymakers have pushed in other directions. Some policies have sought to let markets run riot—especially across borders. But the idea that markets frequently fail and government must step into the breach is among the most widely held in U.S. political economy and often the one that emerges victorious. Indeed, Naidu, Rodrik, and Zucman are so dedicated to the standard model of describing and correcting market failures that Rodrik's own proposal is "distinctive" from the others because he "gives an explicitly pro-social justification for restrictions on trade, not trying to clothe the protectionism in terms of ameliorating some other externality or market failure."

What has tended to separate left and right in responding to market failures is disagreement not over their existence, but rather over government's capacity to respond effectively. Naidu, Rodrik, and Zucman exhibit little interest in this countervailing possibility of government failure, instead lamenting that "even when some economists recognize market failures, they worry government action will make things worse." A call to solve market failures without concern for government failures is not economics *after* anything; it is economics dug into a trench on the frontlines of a thirty-year political war.

The project's potential power, then, comes not from its reaffirmation of the market's fallibility, but from its redefinition of the market's ends. Its call for an "inclusive prosperity" is laudable, as is its demand that we "consider the whole distribution of outcomes, not simply the average (the 'middle class'), and that we consider human prosperity broadly, including nonpecuniary sources of well-being." Hear, hear. This statement of public policy's objective confronts a view that has dominated economics and policymaking across the political spectrum in recent decades—one characterized by an obsession with optimizing consumer welfare through growth and redistribution of the so-called economic pie. *How* best to grow the pie, and *how much* to redistribute, were the focus of debate. But massive helpings of pie were the unquestioned goal. Call it "economic piety."

If that economic piety is the true gravamen of "neoliberalism," then a consensus does exist that requires moving beyond, and "Economics After Neoliberalism" can stake its claim. With a different notion of prosperity would come different modes of evaluation, different failures, and thus different policies. But here the second issue emerges: the traditional tools of economics do not answer the political question of what goals a society should orient itself toward. When maximizing consumer welfare is the name of the game, economists can find market failures and suggest fixes. But who names the game?

Naidu, Rodrik, and Zucman could have defined and defended a substantive vision toward which they orient their economics. Instead, they present their values as neutral and self-evident, offering, for instance, three examples of "nonpecuniary sources of well-being": "from health to climate change to political rights." Those are all important issues, but they evince a very specific outlook. They are the same three issues, in that order, given top billing on Pete Buttigieg's campaign website in early July. But are the pride and dignity of fulfilling duties, supporting a family, and contributing to a community also sources of nonpecuniary well-being? If so, where would those priorities sit next to Buttigieg's? What about the close intergenerational bonds of an extended family or the traditions of a tight-knit community?

Of course, any list of values would be incomplete, but a well-crafted one should call to mind the types of concerns included or excluded. The homogeneously progressive mindset implied by Naidu, Rodrik, and Zucman's initial list is confirmed by the authors' own construction of "justice-efficiency," which defines "justice" as the value to be balanced with efficiency. Justice is an important value, of course, but its assertion as the primary one is a progressive predilection, not a universal truth. Many people would give priority to liberty, or tradition, or the strength of families and communities. Note also that, after investing in the idea that prosperity requires a nonpecuniary definition, the authors have already returned the term to its role as a synonym for efficiency. Adopting the lens of a justice-efficiency frontier, the project becomes an effort to temper the traditional economic emphasis on efficiency with a progressive vision of justice, presented with the patina of "an empirical orientation, an experimental mind set, and a good dose of humility to recognize the limits of our knowledge."

One of the project's accompanying essays on social insurance and childhood investment provides a practical illustration: it claims strong theoretical and empirical support for the argument that public funding of childcare would improve "welfare," but it never defines the term. No commentary contemplates whether children have higher "welfare" when placed in daycare centers than when raised by a parent at home, whether parents have higher "welfare" when given large government benefits contingent on leaving their kids in daycare and going back to work, or whether communities are better off when households all make that choice. What is raising a child, or being raised by a parent, worth?

The fact that the larger project seems to carefully curate and validate progressive policies is peculiar, because the argument would surely be much richer, its audience broader, and its implications more startling if it could do more than reinforce a partisan agenda. Immigration would be an especially obvious topic to tackle—recall that, on trade, the framework supports an "explicitly pro-social justification for restrictions"—yet the topic gets no mention beyond vague laments about "nativism" and those "stuck at home." Free college gets multiple nods, but focus could have gone toward the sizable share of the population that would benefit from other bridges between high school and productive work. Balancing environmental protection with the interests of blue-collar workers would also be ripe for exploration.

"Economics After Neoliberalism" may play a useful role in politics during neoliberalism. But economics after neoliberalism will hopefully fall farther from the tree.

Cass

IN DEFENSE OF NEOLIBERALISM
William Easterly

SINCE COMPLAINTS about the domination of market fundamentalism seem to greatly outnumber pro-fundamentalist manifestos, Naidu, Rodrik, and Zucman may have trouble finding debate partners who will defend ideological, fundamentalist, fetishist neoliberalism. As a personal favor to the authors, whom I like and respect, I will volunteer to be at least a neoliberal—I hope to be excused from the other labels.

Naidu, Rodrik, and Zucman have done a valuable service with their initiative; the policy debate should be expanded because there is danger in neglecting inequality. And yes, there are some government interventions that would improve equality while not destroying the benefits of markets. But there are dangers also in the other direction. Rejecting markets too much, I will argue, can hurt material well-being, individual rights, and the fight against xenophobia.

There is, quite simply, too much straw-manning going on in this debate. Market fetishism implies laissez-faire with no role for government, while market criticism gets unfairly associated with the

North Korean approach to inequality. Both sides talk only about the danger in one direction and not the other. It would be far more useful for both sides to identify just how far they would stop short of either extreme on the North Korea/laissez-faire continuum.

Naidu, Rodrik, and Zucman likely agree that there are numerous examples of disaster when extreme policies inhibit market functioning. By 1982, for example, Ghana had lost its historic domination of the world cacao market after centralized control meant that Ghanaian cacao exporters received only 6 percent of the world price of cacao. With so little incentive to produce, there were not many cacao exporters left. Moreover, those who tried to smuggle their product out of the country in order to find better prices faced the death penalty. This was but one example of the draconian controls of markets in Ghana that are associated with a steep decline in living standards in the decades after independence in 1957. After a drought in 1983 made things even worse, economic reforms to liberalize markets finally began—reforms that have been associated with healthy, positive growth.

This is a familiar story—indeed, one that gets to the heart of why many economists tend to believe in markets. In the 1980s and 1990s, in Latin America and Africa, extreme policies on inflation, interest rate controls, foreign exchange controls, artificial exchange rates, and international trade used to be common—and growth was poor. Now, extreme anti-market policies have mostly disappeared, which is correlated with growth recoveries in both Latin America and Africa. (A big exception is Venezuela, where severe price controls have led to starvation.) Even more famously, the movement from a planned economy toward markets in China (though hardly ending up at laissez-faire) is associated with rapid growth and a historic decline in poverty.

Yet this happy news—in Latin America, Africa, and China—could be reversed if reactions against markets go too far. Nor are rich countries immune from harmful policies—just consider a no-deal Brexit, which is expected to cut Britain's exports and gross domestic product. I am not accusing Naidu, Rodrik, and Zucman of supporting extremes, but I do think their initiative could be improved by not casting markets, writ large, as toxic.

Indeed, their real enemy is inequality, and they see fighting it as a moral value. That value is common, but it is not the only one. Some voters also value personal rights and self-determination, while disliking coercion and dictation by others. In Naidu, Rodrik, and Zucman's telling, ideology in economics is bad because it means rigging evidence. I agree, but such biases could conceivably happen from either conservative or progressive ideologies. Moreover, ideological differences need some respect if they are just competing sets of values. Neither side of the markets and inequality debate can impose their values on others.

Naidu, Rodrik, and Zucman also make a passing mention of nativism—how they "were horrified by the illiberal, nativist turn in our politics." This turn, however, was not caused by markets. Indeed, it was the economists who emphasized markets that first gave us the useful insight that the world is not only zero-sum conflict between ethnic groups, nations, or classes. Market exchanges among individuals can often result in mutual gains, a positive-sum game. There are some losers from trade, yes, but there will be many more if

Donald Trump completely rejects the positive-sum games with his trade wars and travel bans. In terms of the continuum, voters in the United States and Europe are not convinced these days about gains from trade, but they are not voting for redistributionist solutions either.

Lastly, Naidu, Rodrik, and Zucman stress and applaud economists' "recent empirical bent." I think they mean empirics that address causality, usually with natural or researcher-induced experiments in which one group randomly gets a policy intervention and the other group does not. But such evidence does not cover the effects of national choices of market or nonmarket systems, where such random experiments are usually not available or feasible. Evidence cannot resolve political conflicts about values; you need to decide where to go before estimating the most effective way to get there.

So, in conclusion, kudos to Naidu, Rodrik, and Zucman for enhancing the debate about markets and inequality. They could enhance the debate even more by emphasizing that inequality is not the only danger in an increasingly dangerous world.

MARKETS ARE POLITICAL
Debra Satz

LIKE NAIDU, RODRIK, AND ZUCMAN, I celebrate the advantages of markets in aggregating information, allocating scarce resources, and promoting growth. I also agree that there is nothing built into the fabric of economic thought that leads to neoliberalism, and that economics has recently taken on a more empirical, less a priori cast. But I part ways in thinking of markets as only economic artifacts. The Economics for Inclusive Prosperity (EfIP) initiative promises to provide the basis for a robust alternative to market fundamentalism by mobilizing the latest insights from contemporary *economics*. But markets raise political and philosophical questions, too, and no strategy for taking on market fundamentalism will be complete without addressing them.

Markets differ in their technical and empirical aspects—whether information is asymmetric, whether firms exhibit monopoly behavior, and so on—but they also differ in how they structure relations of power and shape human development and motivations. Labor markets, as Adam Smith and Karl Marx observed, enable and inhibit various human capacities, a fact that raises different questions than are raised by a market in apples. Treating childcare as just another market good obscures the role of care in cultivating the capacities and ensuring the interests of small children.

Market fundamentalism elides such distinctions. As economist James Tobin wrote, "Any good second-year graduate student could write a short examination paper proving that voluntary transactions in votes would increase the welfare of the sellers as well as the buyers." Market fundamentalism reduces the question of when and where markets are appropriate to the question of market failure. (Any good graduate student in economics could also prove that voluntary transactions in votes have third-party costs and are not efficient!) And its proponents' preferred solution to market failure has been, when possible, to introduce missing markets to enhance efficiency.

To the extent that market fundamentalism has a "political philosophy," it associates markets with a particular idea of freedom. Its proponents embrace the importance of the ability to exit from contractual relationships, the right to choose one's occupation, and the absence of legal restrictions on entry into political and social positions. Finally, markets are seen as the ideal way of organizing social cooperation given that free individuals differ in their fundamental orientations to life and their priorities.

Offering an alternative to market fundamentalism, then, requires articulating not only a more adequate economics, but also a more adequate political philosophy. In particular, we need to explore alternative conceptions of freedom, fairness, and democracy.

The first part of a persuasive response to market fundamentalism involves offering an alternative idea of *freedom*, by showing that the same concerns that lead us to embrace the importance of exit, occupational choice, and formal freedom should lead us to embrace a more substantive idea of freedom. Consider that if one wishes for the poor to be able to compete with the rich for favorable social positions, it is not enough to simply remove *legal* obstacles. Similarly, without a decent fallback position, workers are not really "free" to exit from exploitative work.

In addition, we can and should develop an alternative vision of *fair cooperation*. Market outcomes can produce many good things, but their outcomes need not be fair. "Inclusive prosperity" gestures to one idea of fair cooperation, but there are others. Countering market fundamentalism means challenging the default position of the market, and thinking explicitly about the underlying rules of the game.

Moreover, there are important cases in which we should make decisions democratically, not as separate individuals. Markets allow individuals to cooperate without agreement on ends, and to act on their private desires and interests. But there are occasions when it seems more appropriate for us to deliberate together as citizens, in circumstances where acting separately would have undesirable consequences. Likewise, there are cases in which we have reason to want our interests as citizens to prevail over our interests as consumers or private parties. Evidence indicates, for example, that choice schools in the United States are more homogeneous than public schools with respect to social class and race. As citizens, we have reason to want an education system that integrates students across class and racial lines. To achieve that aim requires acting in common: each parent deciding alone what is the best school for their child will not yield racially and economically integrated schools.

Markets can also conflict with the wishes we have as citizens in the international context. While citizens have an interest in controlling the terms of their association, markets extend beyond national borders. Is it acceptable for a country to place limits on foreign ownership? Restrict immigration? Market fundamentalists have simple answers to these questions. The answers provided by an alternative economics should be complex because the values at stake are complex. I have already called attention to three such values: freedom, fair cooperation, and collective decision-making by citizens over features of their society. These values might be best furthered by significant restrictions on the scope of the market. Consider that the values of fair cooperation and substantive freedom might be best satisfied when health care, education, and childcare are provided as public goods.

It would be naïve to think that collective deliberation on such matters as education and immigration (or property arrangements, or taxation) will yield consensus. Even people who are committed to the three values above disagree about their weight and priority, and there are bound to be disagreements about the appropriate scope and place of such values in our collective life. In many circumstances, compromise, negotiation, voting—in, short politics—will be appropriate.

All this is to say that while I am excited by the launch of the EfIP, I do not think economists can do this all on their own. A significant alternative to the market fundamentalist program has to show that important values can be better served by policies that include not only redistribution, but also predistribution, as well as setting limits to the scope of market allocation in favor of collective democratic decision-making. I hope that insights from other disciplines, including political philosophy and ethics, will be a more explicit part of this project.

WHAT ABOUT DEVELOPING COUNTRIES?

Arvind Subramanian

AFTER NEARLY FOUR YEARS of working as chief economic adviser to the government of India, I find the Economics for Inclusive Prosperity (EfIP) initiative frustratingly peripheral to the concerns of developing countries, especially the poorer among them. Full disclosure: Dani Rodrik is a friend and long-time collaborator on work that challenges aspects of EfIP's paradigm.

To begin with, the EfIP critique responds to problems in *advanced* economies. It is true that in the rich world, the neoliberal model has failed to deliver much of anything besides enormous returns to the rich and decent GDP growth (and even the latter has not always been a given). Productivity growth has slowed to a crawl, median incomes have stagnated, mobility has declined, and inequality has increased sharply. These problems have in turn bred the political pathologies of democratic authoritarianism and illiberal populism.

But in *developing* countries over the past quarter century—the high noon of the neoliberal paradigm—things have largely gone right. As

Justin Sandefur, Dev Patel, and I showed recently, standards of living across the developing world have begun to catch up to those of the rich world in a way that has not happened for centuries. To be sure, this performance is not guaranteed to continue. But the question remains: What is the problem to which the EfIP critique is offering a solution?

The mismatch is most apparent in EfIP's specific policy proposals, aimed at the pitfalls of austerity, secular stagnation, the new focus on "predistribution" (for example, via minimum wage increases) as opposed to traditional redistribution, and the reining in of runaway finance. None of these would feature in the list of policy priorities for the average developing country.

Even on the most important contribution of the EfIP critique—that inclusiveness should be central to the discourse of growth, rather than an afterthought—there are risks for developing countries. This is not because income is distributed more equally there; far from it. But high marginal income taxes and wealth taxes are less feasible and less effective in countries with weak state capacity, which breeds evasion and corruption. Moreover, there is the risk of overcorrection; if the pendulum should swing too far away from a focus on economic growth, progress for the lives of billions will remain limited.

The EfIP agenda also seems to ignore the lessons learned by policymakers in developing countries. It stresses the defects of markets and the virtues of the state, suggesting the perceived imbalance can be restored by reinvigorating the state. It is certainly true that the neoliberal paradigm exaggerated the virtues of markets. But it is also true that the performance of developing countries improved in part because they adopted some (but not all) of the neoliberal paradigm, such as the need to ensure macroeconomic stability and eschew value-destructive policy interventions.

The greatest flaw of the EfIP critique is the dichotomy that it poses—or, perhaps, presupposes—between states and markets. The reality in developing countries is that *both* states and markets are weak. One might say that this is the very condition of underdevelopment. Essential public services are delivered poorly or not at all, while at the same time markets are afflicted with cronyism, inadequate contestability, and excessive concentration of power. When India dismantled the License Raj, for example, in order to allow a greater role for the private sector, some of these markets then developed a concentration of power that reflects a serious regulatory failure on the part of the state itself. Meanwhile, other markets, such as banking and aviation, malfunction because the state is unable to facilitate the exit of the inefficient, politicized public sector incumbents.

As a result, in developing countries the task is not to redress an imbalance between two robust forces—markets on the one hand, states on the other—but to create and strengthen them in the first place. In some sense, this double challenge is unsurprising, for Karl Polanyi pointed out long ago how deeply markets are embedded in the state and other social institutions.

But how can state capacity be improved? This is a mystery. After all, the Indian state has for decades been unable to deliver basic health and education. But the same Indian state has been effective in implementing something as politically, technologically, and administratively complex as the Goods and Services Tax (GST). Similarly, India has been able to regulate capital markets reasonably well, but has had only limited success in regulating pollution. Why the difference? Truth be told, we do not have a clue.

Some time ago, economists hoped the problem would solve itself, at least to some extent, because institutions would improve as incomes rose. But this has not happened with any regularity. Most strikingly, educational outcomes in India have remained flat or even deteriorated, despite 40 years of high GDP growth (often well above 6 percent annually) and soaring private returns to education. I cite India not because it is representative but precisely because it is an outlier. If serious problems of state capacity and institutions persist even after four decades of stellar economic growth, imagine the plight of most countries, which have experienced much less dynamism.

The EfIP agenda would be more compelling to a global audience if it made these issues central to its thinking. In the end, the real contribution of the critique is one of sensibility. Its emphasis on moving from certitudes to openness, narrowness to ecumenicism, and templates and best practice to "it all depends" and "context matters" represents real progress. Humility replacing hubris is unambiguously good news.

But humility may not be enough. Perhaps there is a deeper truth that we are condemned to accept. Economics might well help us understand the world but give us little guidance on how to change it. It may not have much to say on reforming the big things that really matter, such as basic institutions and the markets they support—a task that is central to countless economic and social outcomes. And that seems to be as true of the new critique as it was of the neoliberal paradigm that the brave new warriors are seeking to supplant.

TRADE RESTRICTIONS WILL NOT ACHIEVE ETHICAL GLOBALIZATION

Margaret E. Peters

I WOULD LIKE TO FOCUS on Dani Rodrik's scheme to combat the dark side of "social dumping." His idea is, according to Naidu, Rodrik, and Zucman, "indicative of the commitments of many of the members of EfIP: a willingness to subordinate textbook economic efficiency to other values, such as democratic rule and egalitarian relationships among citizens." Rodrik contends that, to ensure U.S. workers compete on a level playing field without being undercut by practices that would be illegal here, we could restrict trade with countries that violate minimum labor or environmental standards. He proposes public hearings to debate and determine what constitutes unfair trade. These protections, Rodrik argues, would allow us to maintain high standards while at the same time making U.S. businesses more competitive, thus safeguarding jobs. This scheme is unlikely to succeed on some of its central aims. It probably would not protect U.S. jobs, and it would likely hurt the world's poorest countries.

Regarding U.S. jobs, since the end of World War II, governments have made it easier and easier to trade goods and to locate production in any country. Technological development has also made it easier for businesses to replace workers with machines. It is this combination of free trade and automation that has led to steep U.S. job losses in manufacturing.

Along the way, businesses have become less supportive of low-skill immigration. Because many firms can easily move production overseas, immigrant labor at home becomes less important to them. Why would business leaders worry about bringing Mexican workers to the United States when they can take their factories to Mexico? Similarly, businesses that automate production no longer need as many workers, so they too become less invested in immigration. Finally, firms that close due to overseas competition are the ones that tend to employ low-skill workers, including many immigrants, but they are no longer around to support immigration.

This pattern has severely eroded business support for low-skill immigration. Less support, in turn, strengthens the hand of immigration opponents, and policymakers then restrict immigration to appease these groups. Trade restrictions such as those Rodrik proposes could reverse this trend, creating more jobs in U.S. manufacturing. But businesses would not necessarily hire U.S. workers. Instead they are likely to increase their use of technology or lobby for increased immigration and use immigrant workers instead. This is what happened in the United States 150 years ago when Congress enacted tariffs to grow U.S. businesses. Instead of hiring expensive native labor, these businesses were often early adopters of labor-saving technologies and major proponents of relatively open borders. Rodrik's proposal, in short, may boost U.S. manufacturing, but not U.S. jobs.

A major downside of Rodrik's proposal is that, instead of incentivizing governments to increase labor and environmental standards, these protections would likely keep foreign firms from investing in developing nations. Foreign investors do not like uncertainty, and trade barriers with the U.S. would increase uncertainty. This is a problem because many of trade's labor abuses come not with foreign firms but with domestically owned firms that supply global production. International businesses tend to be the most productive businesses that can afford to pay higher wages and follow regulations. Once invested in a developing country, international businesses often push for economic reforms. Domestic firms do not want reform—because they cannot compete if labor costs more—and are often deeply tied to the ruling party, especially in autocracies. Instead of increasing labor standards to attract international capital, many states are likely to protect domestic businesses and let the international firms go elsewhere.

The downside of this situation is that industrialization through globalization has lifted billions of people out of poverty in developing countries in the last fifty years. As countries such as China and India are now becoming middle income, low-skill industries are increasingly picking up and moving to poorer nations such as Indonesia and Bangladesh. They are even beginning to move to some of the least developed nations, as in sub-Saharan Africa. However well intentioned, then, the protections Rodrik proposes are likely to target the least-developed nations by decreasing foreign investment, and may unintentionally harm those who are worse off in the world.

What is the alternative? Instead of implementing trade restrictions, we could welcome more low-skill immigration. This would help protect our high labor standards and spread them abroad.

First, a wealth of evidence has shown that immigrants do not compete with low-skill Americans for jobs; instead, they *complement* native workers. Most jobs require both routine or manual tasks and tasks that need country-specific knowledge, such as language facility or cultural understanding. Immigrants rarely have the country-specific knowledge to outcompete natives for such jobs.

Second, as Rodrik suggests, many of the labor abuses that come with immigration occur because immigrants have precarious legal status. When their visas depend on their employers (or when they are undocumented), immigrants are unlikely to complain about their employers' violations of labor laws and other regulations. Giving low-skill immigrants more secure status would help combat this problem.

More immigrants are likely to provide more employment for natives, too. Immigrants spend money on housing, food, clothing, health care, and the like. Such spending increases demand for goods and services provided in the United States. More immigrants would also make U.S.-produced goods cheaper for export, since expensive native labor could be deployed more effectively. This would come at a relatively low cost for the nation: legal immigration would increase the nation's coffers, as it would help ensure employers would withhold taxes. (Even now, 50 to 75 percent of undocumented immigrants pay their income taxes.)

Low-skill immigration is also good for immigrants themselves and for their communities. Immigrants are able to earn more money than they would at home and often share that prosperity back home through remittances. Money is not the only thing they share, either. They also learn democratic values, including support for labor unions, which help ensure labor standards at home. As I show in a paper with Michael Miller, greater immigration to the United States can lead to democratization, and more protection for labor, back home.

The one thing that more immigration may not do is to solve the *cultural* problem of globalization. U.S. attitudes toward free trade are often based on enthocentrism. Many Americans, including those that Rodrik is worried about, object to trade precisely because it is associated with foreigners. More low-skill immigration may exacerbate these tensions, at least in the short run.

And yet, U.S. attitudes toward immigrants are changing. More and more people view immigrants and immigration, and by extension foreigners, positively. This is especially true for young people who have grown up around many first- and second-generation immigrants. More immigration, then, may get us to think more as world citizens than only as U.S. citizens. Likewise it may provoke more mass participation, regionally and globally, that will advance the fight for global labor standards.

INCLUSIVE PROSPERITY FOR GLOBAL SUPPLY CHAINS

Alice Evans

STRONG, INDEPENDENT LABOR MOVEMENTS have always been critical to inclusive prosperity. By organizing large-scale, disruptive strikes, workers can secure better pay. The United States, for example, has recently experienced a wave of teacher strikes in which teachers have effectively resisted public education cuts, secured better pay, and inspired hope. Through successful activism, many teachers have become emboldened, realizing they *can* influence wage negotiations.

Unions work, now and historically. Yet U.S. union membership is at an all-time low, which curbs union efficacy. Without harnessing their strength in numbers, workers struggle to secure wage hikes and resist anti-union legislation. The vicious cycle then perpetuates hopelessness, further discourages unionization, and compounds inequality.

What can be done? In his policy proposal, Suresh Naidu argues that workers' proclivity to unionize is a cost-benefit analysis. He proposes clever ways to increase the benefits and lower the costs of collective action. Unions could recruit more members by providing valued training and financial rewards, by convincing influential workers, and by raising expectations of wider support. Unions could also increase their efficacy by targeting financial entities higher up the value chain (similar to the Justice for Janitors campaign), by prohibiting employers from hiring replacement workers, and by mandating that the benefits of automation be shared with all workers. If unions were more effective and membership was more beneficial, then U.S. workers would be more likely to join. Absolutely.

But what about the workers making our clothes, shoes, and electronics in global supply chains? They face even larger obstacles to organization: anti-union legislation, hostile bureaucracies, dismissals, blacklisting via biometrics, brutal police, hired thugs, and little hope of success. The governments of low- and middle-income countries often repress labor to keep costs down and maintain export competitiveness. As U.S. companies scour the world for low costs, exporters try to boost competitiveness by cutting corners on safety, curtailing labor inspectorates, and neutering trade unions. And when one government quashes workers' freedom of association and collective bargaining rights, its economic competitors tend to follow suit.

So how can we tackle labor repression in global supply chains? The short answer is global economic incentives, so that labor repression ceases to be a competitive export strategy. Once governments adopt prolabor reforms, domestic activists become less fearful and mobilize for substantive change.

Consider what happened in Vietnam while negotiating the Trans-Pacific Partnership (TPP). Before TPP, the government of Vietnam prohibited independent trade unions. Even though some members of the party-state and wider civil society were privately supportive of independent unions, they stayed quiet for fear of repercussions. Without seeing public dissent, others doubted the possibility of political change.

The United States insisted that Vietnam allow independent unions if it wanted to join TPP. Because Vietnamese leaders desired increased market access, it became politically acceptable to openly discuss independent trade unions. Top-down authorization reduced fears of reprisals and legitimized more open discussions. Reformists became more vocal, realized wider support for independent unions, and became emboldened to further their preexisting agenda. This fostered a positive feedback loop, culminating in a resolution to permit independent trade unions.

That is where the good news ends. Reform stalled when the economic incentives rescinded. Following Donald Trump's election, the United States withdrew from TPP. Without the incentive of increased market access, the government of Vietnam put legislative change on hold, reversed earlier liberalization, passed new legislation punishing dissent (much like China's surveillance laws), and detained independent activists. Vietnamese NGOs now struggle to gain government approval.

Global economic incentives also incentivized prolabor reforms in Bangladesh. The Rana Plaza factory collapse in 2013 killed over a thousand garment workers and triggered international outcry.

The government of Bangladesh feared buyers would flee en masse. The EU threatened trade sanctions, and the Obama administration suspended Bangladesh's trade privileges. To salvage its reputation and preserve export growth, the government of Bangladesh announced a series of prolabor reforms, including allowing workers to unionize without disclosing their list of supporters to factory owners.

Domestic activists seized on this political liberalization, registering 228 new unions between 2013 and 2014. Unions also strengthened their organizational skills, recruiting new members, securing trust, collecting fees, strengthening internal democracy, and experimenting to overcome management repression. Feeling "hopeful," over 50,000 garment workers went on strike in September 2013 (5 months after Rana Plaza) and secured a minimum-wage hike.

But prolabor reforms were contingent upon global economic incentives. Despite the government's fears, exports actually grew after Rana Plaza. U.S. firms continued to source from Bangladesh with only a minority signing onto health and safety initiatives. Many turned a blind eye to abuses and continued to squeeze prices.

As global economic incentives shifted, the government resumed labor repression, refusing to register trade unions. By 2016 the government was rejecting nearly half of union applications in Dhaka. In December of that year, garment workers went on strike again to call for a higher minimum wage. (Minimum wage is currently $63 a month, among the lowest in the global garment industry.) Sixteen hundred workers were fired, and thirty-five labor organizers and workers arrested. Seeing violent repression, many workers became despondent and stopped trying to unionize. Just last month, at another demonstration for higher wages, police fired rubber bullets and tear gas. One garment worker was killed, 50 were injured, and 11,600 lost their jobs. Without a strong labor movement, real wages continue to fall.

Going forward, we need to *entrench* prolabor incentives in global supply chains, so that labor repression is no longer conducive to export competitiveness. One policy option is Dani Rodrik's antisocial dumping scheme; another is corporate accountability. Without corporate accountability, we have corporate impunity.

But change is afoot. In France all large companies must reduce risks of human rights and environmental abuses in their supply chains—or else be liable. In 2018 the Swiss National Council voted for similar legislation. The German Ministry of Economic Cooperation recently announced a draft law. Politicians in Finland, Germany, and Luxembourg have called for EU-wide regulation.

Corporate accountability might incentivize more scrupulous sourcing, making prolabor reforms and inclusive prosperity more economically competitive export strategies.

A TRANSDISCIPLINARY APPROACH

Complexity Economists

(Eric Beinhocker, W. Brian Arthur, Robert Axtell, Jenna Bednar, Jean-Philippe Bouchaud, David Colander, Molly Crockett, J. Doyne Farmer, Ricardo Hausmann, Cars Hommes, Alan Kirman, Scott Page, and David Sloan Wilson)

WE WELCOME NAIDU, RODRIK, AND ZUCMAN's contribution and the debate it has inspired. We share much of their agenda for an economics "beyond neoliberalism," in particular their emphasis on more empiricism, greater policy relevance, an increased focus on economic inclusion, and a broader notion of prosperity. We are also heartened by their calls to turn away from "market fetishism"; to reintroduce concerns about economic, social, and political power; and to take a more systemic, less siloed view of the economy.

Nonetheless, we believe that Naidu, Rodrik, and Zucman do not go far enough in their calls for reform. The vision they paint is still focused on the discipline of economics and anchored in the core ideas of neoclassical theory that dominated the field in the twentieth century. We believe that in order for economics to progress, it needs to fully embrace a transdisciplinary approach and modernize a number of its key concepts.

Our backgrounds are in economics, political science, psychology, anthropology, physics, computer science, evolutionary theory, and complex systems theory. To us, the phenomenon called "the economy" is a highly complex, multilevel system that encompasses human biology, human behavior, group behavior, institutions, technologies, and culture, all mutually entangled in networks of nonlinear, dynamic feedback. Each of these levels in the system is subject to learning, adaptation, evolutionary, and coevolutionary processes, which means that the system is constantly changing, self-creating, and never at rest. These dynamics in turn create system-level emergent behaviors, including economic growth, inequality, and financial booms and busts. The whole system, in turn, is deeply embedded in the physical processes of our planet.

This transdisciplinary perspective, sometimes referred to as "complexity economics," differs in a number of significant ways from the traditional perspective of economics. We will give three examples.

First, Naidu, Rodrik, and Zucman correctly note that the behavioral economics critique of the rational actor model has become mainstream. Yet despite this, much economic modeling, including much policy modeling, continues to use rational choice assumptions. There remains a perception that rational choice is a "good enough approximation" and that there is no acceptable alternative model—as economist George Stigler said, "it takes a model to beat a model." But if economists widened their view to include neuroscience, cognitive science, anthropology, social psychology, evolutionary biology, computer science, and philosophy, they would see that, over the last few decades, there has been a revolution in behavioral science that should have a major impact on economics.

The picture that this work paints of *Homo sapiens* looks almost nothing like *homo economicus*. Instead of asocial, transactional, self-regarding utility maximizers, real humans are intensely social, highly cooperative, and other-regarding creatures who make decisions inductively, heuristically, mimetically, and through group reasoning. Evolution has given us a repertoire of tools to help us successfully navigate life in groups: these include hormonal responses that trigger caring instincts; neural capacities that vicariously experience the welfare of others; and behavioral strategies for reciprocity, cooperation, and punishment of those who violate group norms. These emotions and behaviors have in turn coevolved with cultural norms, including our moral norms.

A large body of empirical and experimental work shows that moral and social considerations strongly shape economic and political preferences. These preferences often do not align with standard economic views about self-interest, incentives, and "rationality." For example, many progressives have been stumped as to why so many of Donald Trump's voters would take positions that appear to be against their so-called self-interest. Yet, to researchers studying moral psychology, Trumpian narratives on social spending, immigration, trade, and climate change all use a common frame of reciprocity violations that stimulates moral outrage and motivates collective behavior. The typical progressive strategy of appealing to self-interest (cuts in social spending will hurt you, immigration and trade are good for the economy, climate change is bad) is thus doomed to fail because people are not processing these issues in narrow self-interested cost-benefit terms, but rather as issues of moral fairness. Only when progressives begin addressing issues in those terms will they stand a chance of reconnecting with these voters.

A second example of how the complexity economics perspective differs is in its views on heterogeneity. Through most of the twentieth century, economics was primarily concerned with aggregate data such as GDP, productivity, and national income, and the resulting macro-economic models assumed that all of the households and firms in the economy can be summed up as "representatives." These models, which are still in use today, simply ignore heterogeneity. Differences are assumed to come out in the wash, while aggregates and averages are prioritized. Under this view, issues such as economic inequality might matter for social justice reasons, but not for economic reasons. It is not surprising then that both academics and policymakers were blindsided by the tectonic effects of the U-turn in U.S. inequality that began in the 1970s, and its eventual contributions to the 2008 financial crisis. Naidu, Rodrik, and Zucman correctly note that there has been a recent renaissance in work on inequality and many of the Economists for Inclusive Prosperity (EfIP) have made important contributions to this research. Yet much of this work is coming three decades after the fact, looking backward empirically and asking, "what happened?" Economics has yet to grapple with the harder question of how to integrate heterogeneity into its theoretical core and into the models used by policymakers to better answer the questions "why did it happen?" and "what do we do?"

In contrast, explicitly modeling heterogeneity is central to the complexity economics agenda. Borrowing tools widely used in physics, biology, and computer science (e.g., agent-based modeling, network theory, and techniques using micro-level data), researchers are able to model economic systems from "the bottom up"—starting with individual households or workers, fully capturing their key dimensions of difference. For example, how might a policy impact a low-income single mother of two who pays rent, versus a dual-earner, middle-income family with a child in college and a mortgage? And how might the same policy impact the overall macroeconomy? Such approaches have the potential not only to give deeper insights into the causes of phenomena such as inequality, but also to bring political economy back into the heart of economics in a rigorous way.

Finally, a third area of difference is the systems-level view of the economy. Economics has historically assumed that the economy is an equilibrium system—a system at rest. This is a legacy of the ideas and tools economists had available to them in the late nineteenth and early twentieth centuries, but we can do better in the twenty-first. Leading up to the 2008 crisis, for example, central banks used models that operated from the assumption of equilibrium, which made it far less likely that they would see the potential for disaster. In contrast, complex systems approaches can help identify endogenous systemic instabilities and inherent fragilities that can arise in competitive markets. Since the crisis, a number of central banks have been at the forefront in experimenting with non-equilibrium approaches for policy analysis.

An even more disturbing example is climate change. The standard economic view is to see climate change as a cost-benefit problem to be solved using optimization models that "internalize the externality" through carbon prices. This framing has led to an inbuilt bias for cautiousness and delay; as one physicist put it, we may optimize our way to mass extinction. Complexity economics provides an alternative framework. Instead of portraying the environment as an externality, it depicts it as a complex system embedded within the larger complex system of the environment. And it portrays the shift to a zero-carbon economy not as marginal, but as an epochal system transformation on par with the Industrial Revolution or the shift from hunting and gathering to agriculture. It is a problem that requires extremely rapid responses that go far beyond what the standard optimization models even consider, including major changes in our technologies, institutions, behaviors, and cultures. This is the mother of all disequilibrium problems and will require economists to work closely with other disciplines and be open to radically different ways of thinking.

While economists today do use a variety of models, they have historically been drawn from a fairly narrow methodological and conceptual toolbox. Naidu, Rodrik, and Zucman have already done much to broaden the bounds of this toolbox. Our point is to encourage the field to go further, faster. Economics needs to embrace what other fields have learned about behavior, networks, institutions, culture, evolution, and nonequilibrium systems. To date the infrastructure of the economics profession—journals, funding bodies, hiring and tenure committees—has been largely closed to these ideas and approaches. If economics is to reform and move beyond neoliberalism, this needs to change. Only then will we witness the "creative ferment" that Naidu, Rodrik, and Zucman call for.

"ILLIBERAL" ECONOMICS

Caleb Orr

"ECONOMICS AFTER NEOLIBERALISM" describes an economics that uses public power to solve public problems. In other words, it is political economy. This does not mean that it is not "economics." To the contrary, it means that Naidu, Rodrik, and Zucman have revealed an important truth about the discipline. By using economics as a technical tool to achieve public priorities, they demonstrate the inevitability of value decisions and create new possibilities for a politics willing to embrace it.

Economics without politics denies important realities about public life. Real-world developments driven by social and political motivations are chalked up in its models as "market failures" and "asymmetries." It assumes the righteousness of its underlying framework of an equilibrium chosen by the preferences of market participants against other explanations that are understood to be ad hoc or irrational. Making this the basis for public policy is, to use our term for discussion, "neoliberalism"—its own kind of politics.

These assumptions limit a more complete use of economics. A nearly endless series of trade-offs accompanies every significant policy decision. Properly identifying or quantifying these trade-offs for economic purposes requires a hierarchy of values for them to be discovered, sorted, and prioritized. For example, recent studies have identified the inability of workers' skills and experience to transfer between sectors as a significant labor market "adjustment cost" of expanded trade. But why is the labor market, instead of the expanded trade, presumed to be the source of the cost? Workers who have built up years of institutional knowledge and located their families in particular regions should not be expected to adapt well to conditions that require them to start over. The frictions caused by the expectation that market equilibrium requires workers to start over are so numerous and inherent that it might be more appropriate to flip the burden of proof and make "adjustment costs" the primary institutions of analysis, instead of the purported market benefit they serve.

The alternative Naidu, Rodrik, and Zucman propose is to understand political and social qualities such as these as the "embedded . . . institutional prerequisites" behind every supply or demand curve. While including these prerequisites is necessary for any economic analysis, they require a normative evaluation to be fully understood. What does our economy currently produce? What should it produce? How do we facilitate development in this direction? For labor market "adjustment costs," how did the decision to expand trade affect the character of the economy? As Philip Pilkington has written, accepting this necessity should make economics less like a "science" and more like "an exercise in social logistics."

Where neoliberalism can only observe public problems related to the operating of market processes ex post facto, economics after neoliberalism begins with the problems and builds or changes institutions in order to solve them.

An economics proceeding from this insight should liberate the political right to pursue its own goals more thoroughly just as much as it energizes progressive economists. The possibility that economics after neoliberalism could help identify and resolve problems that Naidu, Rodrik, and Zucman reject as an "illiberal, nativist turn" provides new policy grounds to consider and reveals a contradiction in the essay's application of their proposal.

Consider reductions in life expectancy, one of the problems their essay raises. This would be more precisely described as a decline in *male* life expectancy and should be seen alongside the underemployment of working-age men in the U.S. economy. The reduced availability of jobs providing remunerative and geographic stability for men has profound effects on health and well-being for men, as well as entire families. For example, the loss of such jobs means that young adult men in particular are less marriageable and delay or forego family formation, contributing to falling rates of fertility and reduced social stability for men and women alike. Service sector employment often does not compare in terms of stability, productivity, and value-chain position, even if pay remains nominally constant.

Many of the social problems ascribed to globalization, automation, and resultant reduction in manufacturing jobs find their sources in how they have changed the working lives of men and their families. An economics that prioritizes solving this public problem would evaluate trade-offs not often considered by critics of neoliberalism on the left. For example, it would understand the economic effects of low-skill immigration not by the increases in consumer demand created by new earners in the market, but by their composition of employment and who they compete with. Or perhaps it would understand the receipt of cash welfare and refundable tax credits not by their ability to increase purchasing power, but to motivate or sustain labor force attachment.

Consider also the composition of business investment. The rise of business investment in financial and intangible assets rather than physical capital, such as equipment and machinery, has stunted U.S. economic development. Financialization earns profits by lending money to other sectors to invest, instead of the business sector making profits by its own investment. Digitalization earns profits through its ability to earn rents off of platforms that often extract more value from consumers than they create. In other contexts, we would call this kind of private gain at public expense "arbitrage," but it has come to characterize the norm.

Value-neutral markets make no distinction between normal growth and "growth" that destroys productive capacity. Solving this problem will require valuing development itself, like what John Kenneth Galbraith once described as "technical progressivism for its own sake." The considerations that should follow from this goal include those that are typically non-neoliberal, of course, like understanding the shortsightedness of businesses speculating on financial assets. But they may also lead to uncomfortable choices for left critics of neoliberalism. Industrial development is inextricable from national security. Doing it well will look more like competing in new space races with China than decarbonizing old factories. Productivity is its orienting value, not equity or social justice. The primary aim of industrial policy is better-organized capital, not the universal empowerment of labor.

If this pattern of identification is considered "right wing," then economics after neoliberalism clearly supplies the right with new material tools to promote its vision of the common good. Neoliberalism constrained the right's use of positive law in economic policy to areas sufficiently "outside" of the market, for example in the requirement of full-time work for welfare recipients. The framework proposed by Naidu, Rodrik, and Zucman to define economic policy as the provision of public goods would expand this justification to new areas. Work requirements on welfare imply the availability of productive work for its recipients. Pro-family cultural values imply an economy conducive to family formation. Corporate tax cuts imply a requirement to invest capital in the physical economy. Public benefit requires public obligation.

That critics of neoliberalism on the political left might object to the policy implications of these priorities reveals an important possibility—and a contradiction. Economics after neoliberalism could be worse for their stated goals than the economy during neoliberalism. Progressive social causes have become the lingua franca of consumer marketing for large corporations. The management of consumption patterns that sustain corporate earnings requires the creation of new tastes and the liberation of purchasing power for them. Social change can make for profitable business. On climate, the rise of digital technology giants as the national champions of the neoliberal economy provides the most significant example yet of commercial viability without physical economy presence. On inequality, large-scale transfer programs that ensure purchasing power parity across incomes are entirely consistent with neoliberal market institutions, and indeed have expanded during the same period of market liberalization described by the essay. If progress by these standards comes to be understood as political instead of natural, it may very well be changed by democratic society.

Therein lies the contradiction. The right may yet break with neoliberalism more than the left will. In their presumption of the righteousness of their goals and exclusion of certain technical tools from use, Naidu, Rodrik, and Zucman reveal they have not dealt with this possibility. Indeed, if the consideration of substantive values such as the primacy of family formation is denied because it violates a procedural norm, then we are right back where we began. Avoiding value decisions on the grounds that they are "illiberal"—not because they are wrong or technically infeasible—denies the essentially political framework that the economics proposed by the essay requires. "Economics After Neoliberalism" demonstrates this much; for that it should be applauded, and then put to better use.

THE PERILS OF QUANTIFICATION
Ethan Bueno de Mesquita

ECONOMICS STANDS DEEPLY COMMITTED to quantification, especially in its most policy-facing branches. Indeed, a particular approach to quantification for policy analysis is what many applied economists mean by *economics*. This dogma of quantification creates perils for policy that are, in my view, as significant as the market fundamentalism the EfIP authors highlight. As economists rethink the relationship between their discipline and public policy, they would be well served grappling with these issues.

In a textbook vision of policy analysis, quantification is simply a tool; it measures and scores policy alternatives rather than shaping the alternatives themselves. We are invited to think of quantification as in service of policy aims that are defined elsewhere and by others. But this view, while popular, is misleading. We cannot divide the world into a neat dualism of aims and tools. How and what we quantify shapes and determines the aims of public policy, just as those aims shape and determine what we quantify.

The fiction that quantification is some wholly technocratic undertaking underlies three perils of quantification: it flattens the normative standards we use to evaluate policy; it distorts the incentives of those who make and implement policy; and it narrows our field of vision, limiting the policy problems we acknowledge exist or can be addressed.

First, though, an affirmation. Quantification is essential because it creates a framework of contestability. When costs, benefits, and values are quantified, the terms of debate and standards of evidence are clear—which is critical for democratic accountability and good governance. But quantification is not perfect, and we must look its limits squarely in the face.

Despite the rich panoply of normative standards considered by moral and political philosophers, essentially all quantitative policy analysis is rooted in welfarism, the view that policies should be evaluated based on their implications for human well-being. Moreover, the welfarist standard that predominates is what I call *crass* utilitarianism: it defines well-being largely in terms of *material* costs and benefits, such as economic prosperity, health, and other factors for which willingness to pay is straightforward to measure.

Crass utilitarianism lends itself easily to quantitative analysis. While it is hard to quantify the value of rights, duties, or equity, crass utilitarianism is so easy to work with that it has become part of the "standard assumptions" in the background of applied economic thinking. As a result, today we are often not only crass utilitarians, we are unreflective crass utilitarians. The process of trying to maximize net utility—ignoring questions of rights, duties, responsibilities, equity, dignity, and so on—is so ingrained in our practice and thought that we simply take for granted that a good policy is one that optimizes material benefits.

Here we see how misleading the textbook vision is. The aims of public policy are deeply entwined with quantification. We don't quantify because we are utilitarians. We are utilitarians because we quantify. As Michel Foucault put it, utilitarianism has ceased to be a philosophy; it has become "a technology of government."

The next peril of quantification is that it distorts incentives. Typically, we can only quantify a few of the many inputs that go into addressing a social problem. And incentives tend to follow measurement. If we want to hold teachers accountable, and the only thing we can measure is test scores, then a natural line of thinking is, "let's give teachers incentives if their students' test scores improve." The problem is that incentivizing only quantifiable tasks can create perverse distortions in behavior, such as incentivizing teachers to "teach to the test" while neglecting harder-to-quantify skills, such as conflict resolution, self-control, and creative thinking. This distortion can create overall outcomes that are worse than the scenario with no incentives. This problem is, of course, not limited to education policy.

The final peril of quantification, a narrowed field of vision, is in some sense a consequence of the previous two. Many policies create short-run costs for the small number of people alive today, but long-run benefits for the vast number of people who make up future generations. The most obvious example is interventions limiting carbon emissions to prevent global warming. Such policies pose two challenges to any welfarist quantifier. First, if we believe that all people should be treated equally in cost-benefit analyses, we ought to be spending almost all of our current resources on policies that benefit future generations. Second, since policies that affect the future affect such a vast number of people, comparison is hard. Everything looks either infinitely good or infinitely bad.

Quantitative policy analysis responds with a technical fix, called "discounting the future." This idea is inspired by, but distinct from, the financial concept of the time value of money. Say you would be indifferent between receiving 90 cents today or a dollar a year from now. Then the value of money you will acquire in a year is discounted by 0.9, and this diminution continues exponentially as we go further into the future. Cost-benefit analysis extends this methodology to discount future generations' welfare because doing so solves the quantifier's problem of infinite future benefits by writing off the distant future.

But something is suspect here. Yes, I value money for me in the future less than money for me in the present. But, other than the small chance the world will end, why should we value people in the future less than people in the present? Frank Ramsey—who in the 1920s laid the intellectual foundations for thinking rigorously about intertemporal considerations —understood this. He argued that discounting the welfare of future generations "is ethically indefensible and arises merely from the weakness of the imagination." If we do not discount future generations we cannot get on with the business of quantifying benefits and cost. So, here again, the dictate to quantify shapes our normative standards, perhaps without our even noticing.

Quantification also narrows our field of vision by distorting incentives—pushing policy makers to focus on issues that are easily quantified, whether or not those are the most pressing issues. In the United States, for example, the Office of Management and Budget can essentially veto any major regulatory action if it finds the cost-benefit analysis wanting. As a consequence, Lisa Heinzerling, former head of policy at the Environmental Protection Agency, described constantly asking not if something was the right thing for environmental protection, but "How can we make this acceptable to OMB?"

In some sense, of course, this is exactly the goal. If quantification requirements do not change the regulations we get, why have them? The concern, however, is that the mandate to quantify does not simply prevent agencies from promulgating regulations for which the cure is worse than the disease; it discourages work on regulations for which there are good arguments, when quantification is too expensive or impractical.

Perhaps no field of inquiry has had greater impact on policy thought than economics. Quantification, as much as market fundamentalism, underpins that impact. We have been too willing to accept modern quantitative policy analysis as an unalloyed good, without sufficient reflection on the balance of its merits and demerits. This moment of self-examination inspired by Naidu, Rodrik, and Zucman is an opportunity to adjust course. Whether or not quantification's role in policy discourse is ultimately defensible, it has to be defended. I hope that by highlighting some of the perils of quantification, this response might contribute to that process of reflection and reform.

EMPIRICISM'S IMPLICIT BIAS
Marshall Steinbaum

NAIDU, RODRIK, AND ZUCMAN are on the cutting edge of a new era in economics research, one that casts serious doubt on the received wisdom that the "free market" should not be jeopardized through government "intervention." You would be hard-pressed to find an academic economist in good standing now who doubts the essential contingency of economic outcomes. The discipline has largely rejected the simplistic "economics says" pattern of policy prescription—the idea that theory implies we must enact this or that (usually elite-favoring) policy.

But the dead weight of decades of bad economics—and of bad interventions by professional economists in the public debate—remains. In the late 1990s, leading economists advocated for financial deregulation. In the early 2000s, Federal Reserve chairman Alan Greenspan put his great, and unmerited, prestige to work advocating in Congress for regressive tax policy. More recently, in the financial crisis and the global recession that followed, leading members of the economics profession placed their prestige behind the idea that the main threat to the economy was spiraling government debt and a resulting spike in interest rates that would lead to the crowding out of private investment and a stagflation crisis of the type experienced in the 1970s. The fact that these dire warnings repeatedly failed to come true has not stopped a march of bad policies, such as misguided fiscal austerity, from being enacted by politicians who think they are doing what "economics demands" (or so they say).

The public thus has good reason to doubt our lesson, and they will understandably be reluctant to accord a new generation of economists the same level of prestige and deference—particularly if the argument we make about why we should be listened to rests solely on an overly optimistic narrative of scientific progress.

Such narratives have an unfortunate history in the discipline (perhaps in all disciplines). It seems that every new generation proclaims itself to have discovered empirical verification for the first time and is thus in a unique position to enter the policy realm in triumph. In the conclusion to his presidential address to the American Economic Association in 1964, for example, George Stigler announced that "the age of quanitification is now full upon us," and called it "a scientific revolution of the very first magnitude." That shift "has begun to reach public policy, and soon it will make irresistible demands upon us."

Thankfully, Naidu, Rodrik, and Zucman are not nearly as triumphalist as Stigler was. But still they—and the profession at large—must reckon with the significance of this posture. After all, Stigler's research and policy agenda is exactly what Naidu, Rodrik, and Zucman are saying has been shown to be an intellectual dead end from which the field has only just extricated itself, and yet he refers to his agenda in the same tone and rhetoric with which they refer to theirs. This fact tells us that empirical verification and the narrative of progress cannot by themselves accomplish the substantial epistemological and coalition-building work that the EfIP authors seek to place on their shoulders.

The truth is that empirical methods are always laden with assumptions, both of the formal economic-theoretic sort and the more "folk wisdom"–like traditions and methods associated with the discipline's most prominent and powerful members. "Tests" of economic theories are not simple reality checks. We must be on guard against the way they are informed by implicit and unconscious bias and a reflexive defense of mainstream orthodoxy.

Stigler is a case in point. Earlier in that address, he eagerly anticipates the application of economics to the fields of antitrust and common carrier regulation. Yet in the same speech he also explicitly attacks the empirical work of the "German Historical" and "American Institutionalist" scholars, who had a great deal of sway over the introduction of regulatory and antitrust regimes during the New Deal. Scholarship in that tradition was in fact highly rigorous; it was just their ideas that motivated Stigler's criticism. He waged a career-long, successful campaign of vilification against Institutionalist economics, in fact, from the perspective of what he and his collaborators called "Price Theory."

When that approach finally made the leap from the academy and was brought to bear on antitrust and sectoral regulation, starting in the late 1970s, Stigler's theory—that regulation served inefficient incumbents at the expense of innovative entrants, and that anti-trust kept businesses who should properly go out of business in the market—had an enormous impact on policy: the deregulation of the trucking and airline industries in the late 1970s, of telecom in the 1990s, and of finance in the 2000s, as well as the ongoing erosion of antitrust laws at the hands of the federal judiciary, culminating most recently in the 2018 Supreme Court ruling *Ohio v. American Express*. Stigler's enormous intellectual and professional success—a lifelong campaign of academic imperialism, promoted and funded by right-wing interests seeking to roll back the New Deal—dealt immense damage to the body politic and to the public reputation of the economics profession.

But, it turns out, the scholars Stigler vilified were right about how the economy worked. This is but one example of a pattern repeated through the history of the discipline. Economists have drawn and redrawn disciplinary boundaries to exclude anything that challenged incumbent wealth and power, including marginalizing the contri-butions of scholars and would-be scholars from underrepresented communities. The result was to turn the field into a safe space for rich white people to justify and naturalize the status quo.

Another stark example comes from the work and career of economist Abram Harris, who wrote about the banking sector's discrimination against black borrowers—including on the part of black bankers—as a key source of ongoing racial wealth inequality. As a professor at the University of Chicago in 1961, Harris pro-posed to teach an undergraduate course on market power, monopoly, and antitrust policy, and sought to have it listed in the economics department. In response, Stigler privately told the department chair that "the new course . . . arouses no enthusiasm on my part. It sounds like a protracted bull session, in which large ideas are neither carefully analyzed nor empirically tested. . . . My own inclination would be (1) to list it, with explicit proviso that it is only for as long as he teaches it, and (2) advise our majors to forget it."

UNFORTUNATELY, jettisoning Stiglerian methodology is not nearly sufficient to overcome this history of marginalization. For example, in the last several years, a controversy has played out over the impact of so-called "ban the box" regulations, which seek to counter discrimination against the formerly incarcerated by restricting employers (usually in the public sector) from asking about criminal history as part of the job application process. Such legislation draws substantially on the work of sociologist Devah Pager, who documented labor market discrimination against those tainted by past experience with the criminal justice enterprise. Given the high rates of incarceration among young black men, the result is not just individual but group-level discrimination, lasting for a lifetime.

In response, however, several economics researchers concluded that such policies reduce employment opportunities for black men who had never been incarcerated, because in the absence of information to the contrary, employers assume such applicants do in fact have a criminal record and therefore eliminate them from hiring pools. This finding received wide attention in the media and from leading think tanks, fitting as it did into a narrative of misguided do-gooder regulation shown to be counterproductive.

But this revisionist scholarship, which is every bit a part of the empirical revolution Naidu, Rodrik, and Zucman laud, has problems of its own. Research by economist Terry-Ann Craigie actually shows "ban the box" policies operate as intended. This episode reveals that despite the so-called "empirical turn," harmful pathologies remain embedded in the economics profession: the marginalization of underrepresented scholars; the assumption that economists clean up the mistakes made by social scientists from other disciplines; and the eagerness to believe that egalitarian labor market regulations backfire against those they are intended to help.

All of these interlinked tendencies do not dissolve just because we have learned how to run experiments and quasi-experiments, and there is simply no basis in the history of science to think that they would. Justifying racial inequalities and other retrograde scholarly tendencies have always found ways to propagate themselves within whatever the dominant scientific paradigm might be, so economists had best be on the lookout as they wheedle their way into contemporary empirical research.

A final word of caution should inform the work of EfIP: institutional privilege is real. These scholars operate in elite departments, where support for their work is abundant and where threats to their academic freedom may feel remote. That is an increasingly rare thing in U.S. higher education, where successive rounds of state funding cuts have transformed public universities into vulnerable hosts for private parasites. In the face of cuts, administrators go looking for other funding sources to sustain them, and, at least in economics, the open hands tend to come from business funders and right-wing foundations with an agenda of instituting curricula of their own making and of hiring scholars they know will toe the line. I fear that scholars without direct experience of this will be too eager to look to the bright future of a newly enlightened economics profession flush with sophisticated empiricism, without recognizing the threat this right-wing takeover poses to the work of less well-appointed scholars and departments.

I do not mean to detract from the importance of the initiative Naidu, Rodrik, and Zucman have launched. Economics desperately needs a fresh outlook after a decade that has not been kind to our public reputation. Too many economists have reacted defensively to that public condemnation, but these three point in a new and more promising direction: acknowledge that our first loyalty must be to truth, and our second to the public and its welfare. The will to wealth and power has acted on us and on our discipline for too long, and the changing winds are all to the good. Hopefully, when we look back at this moment a decade from now, we will be able to see this as one of a series of steps we took to set the field on a better course.

ECONOMISTS SHOULD ENABLE
DEMOCRATIC PRIORITIES

Suresh Naidu, Dani Rodrik,
& Gabriel Zucman

THE RESPONSES IN THIS FORUM are too insightful to engage with adequately in such a small space. In our attempt to try, however, we have separated the comments into three groups: those that want post-neoliberal economics to be more explicitly normative (Robin, Satz, Bueno de Mesquita, Orr, and Cass); those that ask for greater methodological and institutional pluralism (Complexity Economists, Steinbaum); and those in defense of some version of neoliberalism in the interest of the global poor (Peters, Easterly, and Subramanian).

Alice Evans's essay resists this categorization, but we think it exemplifies the rich institutional and political economy analysis that economists can undertake when they no longer act as public cheerleaders for every form of globalization. We had hoped to spur precisely this kind of thinking about unions, global incentives, and corporate accountability as complementary institutions to promote improved labor conditions in global supply chains and poor countries—though we are perhaps less optimistic than Evans that external forces can be as effective as domestic factors.

TURNING TO THE FIRST GROUP, these writers all identify a tension in our project: we want to promote economists as players in progressive politics, but we never fully articulate a public philosophy to frame and orient the requisite economic analysis. They are right. We want markets to be less hegemonic as institutions and economic arguments to be less pivotal in public discourse, but we do still think economists are a valuable expert community. Rather than oracles channeling a capricious supply-and-demand deity that constrains what democratic government can do, we see economists as enablers of democratic priorities.

We agree with Corey Robin that neoliberalism was created through an intellectual move—one that made the market the arbiter of all other values (e.g., concretely installed in cost-benefit analysis of regulations). If we remove that arbiter, then economists no longer have any particular advantage in divining the values that all members of a society agree on. We fully accept that, as economists, we need to be "modest at the level of public philosophy" (Robin) and to cede ground to our colleagues in other disciplines who have wrestled with complex normative questions (Satz). We recognize that empiricism cannot substitute for normative theoretical frameworks (Bueno de Mesquita). Economists must be more explicit and self-critical about their normative assumptions and, alternatively, not shy about articulating the values that animate their work. There is nothing in mainstream economics that stands in the way of this.

Our conservative critics, Orr and Cass, also ask for more normative content, but substituting conservative for left-wing values. Now that a post-Trump Republican party is less in thrall to its free-market factions, it is unsurprising that conservatives want an economics that allows nonpecuniary values of tradition, authority, and security to be articulated as social goals to be traded off against economic performance. To reiterate, there is nothing in mainstream economics that stands in the way of the emergence of a communitarian conservative view, but to the extent that this view depends on claims about how the world works rather than what is good, it will have to be defended on the basis of peer-reviewed evidence to have standing inside contemporary economics. Trading off EPA regulations against blue collar worker employment is an acceptable position (as the recent Trump Council of Economic Advisors report kind of does), but selectively ignoring the evidence on, for example, infant mortality effects of pollution or costs of climate change is not (as the report also does). Our essay was intentionally aimed at debunking anti-economics stereotypes we encounter on the left, and it is a task for others to exposit modern economics to an audience of conservatives more concerned with family, community, and nation than economic growth.

THE NEXT GROUP OF WRITERS asks economics to be both methodologically and institutionally diverse. In response to the Complexity

Economists, we would say that many of their criticisms have already penetrated mainstream economics. Economists are integrating new approaches to human behavior (from neuroscience to networks to norms) with models of economic decision-making, and they are incorporating a wide variety of heterogeneity into economic models. Heterogeneity has proven central for "noising up" models of general and partial equilibrium, to allow them to account for real-world phenomena. Heterogeneous and distributional impacts of policies (e.g., fiscal and monetary policy, unionization, or taxes) are regularly studied, and macro implications are considered.

We suspect what the authors do not like is the particular analytic tools that economists currently use to handle these issues. Although economists have adopted evolutionary game theory and have incorporated a wide variety of behavioral features into standard models, the benchmark models almost always incorporate agent optimization in some form or another; explicit out-of-equilibrium dynamics are rarely considered. Seeing everything through the lens of constrained optimization is, well, constraining. But it is also quite powerful for thinking about the kinds of intentional behaviors that are distinctive to human interactions. We do not claim that mainstream tools are superior or the only valuable ones—merely that they are useful. We are open to policy analyses that are produced using "complexity economics," and we hope that members of the group will join us in producing them.

As for their charge that mainstream economics is not engaging in "systems thinking," we are doubtful that this is correct. Is everything connected? Yes, obviously, and economists' general equilibrium analysis makes this plenty clear. Indeed, some of the most beautiful economics comes from finding unanticipated connections between social phenomena. Is the best way of analyzing such complicated systems to build computational models with chaotic dynamics? Are there important and well-documented strange attractors in the real economy? We are not sure, but we think it is possible to build on the insights from existing economic models, in addition to developing new frameworks of the "systems"-type.

In his response, Marshall Steinbaum argues that claiming the scientific method as our ally makes us sociologically vulnerable to hierarchical "harmful pathologies" that are embedded in the profession. The elevation of human capital, tastes, and biological comparative advantage in 1960s economics, for example, made it a fertile garden for all of Albert Hirschman's *Rhetoric of Reaction*, with an endless stream of arguments for why attempts to improve the lot of the poorest (or non-white people or women) are doomed to fail or backfire. Not unrelatedly, in socializing prospective economists, economics fetishizes a combative attitude, mathematical prowess, and cultural signifiers of "smarts" in graduate students, creating inhospitable environments for underrepresented minorities and women. This should all be fixed, both institution by institution and in the field as a whole.

But we think the profession's attachment to empirical results is real. The testimonials to the deeply missed Alan Krueger reveal how recent and radical this attachment is. Even as some tributes to Krueger resist his findings (with David Card and Lawrence Katz) that minimum wage increases may not curtail employment, they all acknowledge how deeply influential these findings were for the profession. Earlier economists were not as principled in their commitment to empirical evidence, as evidenced by George Stigler's 1947 dismissal of Richard Lester's survey work on the minimum wage.

Today, theories about how humans interact do not have to be ideological posturing for rich donors nor succor for partisans. We can be committed to the possibility of a pragmatic social science and still see it as a valuable tool for democratic polities. An economics anchored in a diversity of models, with evidence used to sort among them, is better economics. It is not an obviously ideological project. There will be empirical evidence that is inconclusive or eventually proven wrong, and there will be findings that are uncomfortable for both the left and right. As with any historical science, economics needs a proper balance between theory and empirical evidence. The recent movement toward greater empiricism strikes us as moving the discipline closer to the right balance.

OUR LAST GROUP of commentators offer a perspective from economic development and global inequality. While neoliberal economics may be obsolete in the advanced countries, some argue that its basic policy messages have proven to be effective in bringing large groups of desperately poor people into the global middle class. India and China have shown the power of liberalized markets and international trade. Might we be killing the golden goose by suggesting that this was a mistake?

In our view, portraying China and India as neoliberal success stories hides more than it reveals. The key reforms in these cases are reconfigurations of state–economy relationships, far from neoliberal prescriptions. Indeed, if these countries had been failures, there would be no shortage of neoliberal takes today as to why that is so: the state is still too powerful, there is too much industrial policy, trade is not free enough, and so on. Our main argument is that very little of why the policy changes worked can be understood with textbook economics or the first-best benchmarks of the neoliberal economist. One needs to account for pervasive market failures and apply the economics of the second-best.

Margaret Peters pushes us the furthest here and in a most welcome way, articulating the view that (trade and immigration) policy should not be set only in the interest of citizens of rich countries. We would not want a post-neoliberal economics to become an ideological tool for defending the rents of rich citizens against incursions by the poor. We agree with Peters in particular that there should be an increase in low-skill labor flows. But we would also like economists to understand that economic integration is a means and not an end, and that a panoply of institutional arrangements are needed to manage it and keep it politically sustainable. To that end, Rodrik's antisocial dumping proposal (which Peters criticizes) is designed to increase the public legitimacy of trade with developing nations. It is not meant to protect jobs or increase manufacturing employment in the advanced countries. To insist on free trade at all costs would be a pyrrhic victory if it ended up unleashing a wider backlash against economic openness.

Naidu, Rodrik, & Zucman

All of this amounts to the beginning of a much longer conversation —one we look forward to continuing within the Economics for Inclusive Prosperity (EfIP) network, with these respondents, and others.

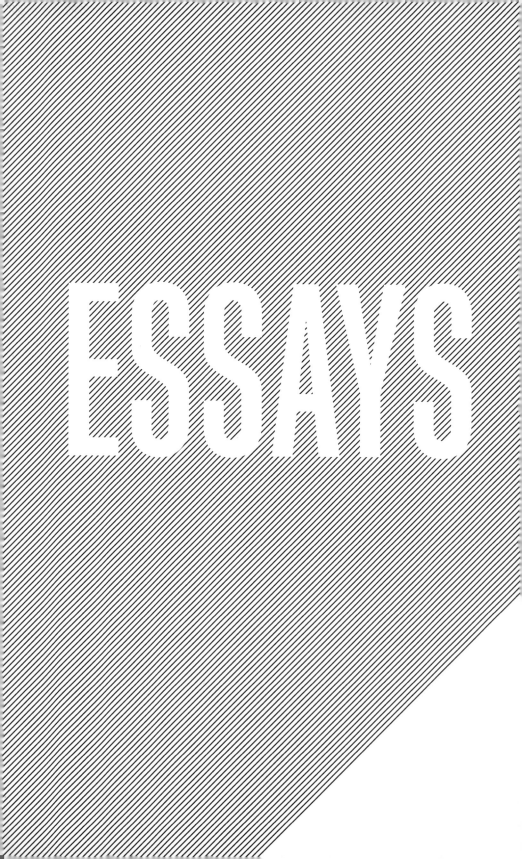

ESSAYS

ESSAYS

SELLING KEYNESIANISM
Robert Manduca

"LET'S BRING OUR EDITORIAL MICROSCOPE into focus on a very significant phenomenon," the video begins. "The middle-income consumer."

As a middle-aged white man comes into view, pushing a wheel-
barrow full of recent purchases, the voiceover chronicles his recent
exploits. "He has fed new demands into the production apparatus of
industry, accounting for the housing boom, appliance sales, the rush
for prepared foods." Altogether, we hear, "the zoom in the American
market after the war, the unprecedented volume of goods of all kinds,
gobbled up by an insatiable tide of buyers, was largely the work of
this middle-income man."

After decades of praise heaped on "job creators," viewers today
may find it disorienting to see the consumer—and a middle-income
one at that—cast as the hero of the economy, instead of the investor or
the entrepreneur. Yet *Fortune*, which produced the video in 1956, was
hardly an outlier. In the mid-twentieth century, advertising, popular
press, and television bombarded Americans with the message that

national prosperity depended on their personal spending. As *LIFE* proclaimed in 1947, "Family Status Must Improve: It Should Buy More For Itself to Better the Living of Others." *Bride* likewise told its readers that when they bought new appliances, "you are helping to build greater security for the industries of this country."

This messaging was not simply an invention of clever marketers; it had behind it the full force of the best-regarded economic theory of the time, the one elaborated in John Maynard Keynes's *The General Theory of Employment, Interest and Money* (1936). The key to full employment and economic growth, many at the time believed, was high levels of aggregate demand. But high demand required mass consumption, which in turn required an equitable distribution of purchasing power. By ensuring sufficient income for less well-off consumers, the government could continually expand the markets for businesses and boost profits as well as wages. Conversely, Keynes's theory implied, growing income inequality would lead to lower demand and slower economic growth.

The basic Keynesian logic of demand-driven growth came to be accepted across U.S. society in large part due to significant postwar efforts to explain, communicate, and popularize it. Proponents of Keynesian thinking worked hard to educate the public about the new economic theory and the possibilities of abundance that it foretold. A particularly compelling example is the book *Tomorrow Without Fear* (1946). Written by Chester Bowles, a former advertising executive turned wartime price czar, it turns Keynes's dry economic theories into accessible and evocative prose. Drawing on the shared experiences of the Depression and World War II, it made the public case for the possibility and the necessity of mass affluence in postwar America.

Similar efforts—other prominent voices included John Kenneth Galbraith and Leon Keyserling—ensured that workers, the popular press, business executives, academic economists, and politicians on both sides of the aisle were largely on the same page: mass consumption among a broad swath of the populace was necessary to a thriving economy. This consensus propelled the fastest sustained rise in output and living standards the United States has ever seen, while also motivating government action to expand social insurance and protect living standards.

Today, as we enter the second decade of recovery from the Great Recession, a growing debate has emerged around new economic ideas, and it remains as important as ever to pay attention to how exactly economic theories win broad public support. By examining the economic beliefs of a more prosperous time—including the popularizing efforts that led to their widespread adoption—we can more fully appreciate how to build new forms of consensus today.

WHAT MOTIVATED PUBLIC INTELLECTUALS, policymakers, and government officials such as Bowles to spend their nights and weekends translating economic theory for the general public? Part of the answer lies in the fact that the experiences of World War II and the Depression forged a unity and clarity of purpose among Americans that can be hard to fathom today. The experiences not only brought existential dread to the country, but also took it from one economic extreme to another.

Manduca

During the 1920s, the government cut taxes and maintained a strict balanced budget in the hopes of sustaining high business confidence and investment. The guiding economic theory held that the primary limit on economic growth was supply (the total amount of labor and capital available). Some economists even thought that an increase in supply would inevitably generate a corresponding growth in demand, a kind of economic equivalent of "if you build it, they will come." But instead of sustained growth, this focus on investment created a bubble that culminated in the biggest bust in history.

Surveying the wreckage, Keynes realized that supply-side thinking got things backward. One glance at the 1930s economy made that clear: everywhere you looked there were recently shuttered factories, along with unemployment rates above 20 percent. Clearly the slump was not due to a lack of capacity to make things, but rather a lack of markets in which to sell them. This is the core Keynesian insight: economic catastrophe can be caused by inadequate demand, which will feed upon itself in a downward spiral. Demand shortfalls often originate with a tightening of investment, as businesses start to worry about having overcommitted. Once that happens, unless the government steps in with fiscal or monetary stimulus, unemployment will follow.

World War II put these ideas to the test, and they passed with flying colors. When the government stepped in and started buying things, U.S. businesses leapt to meet the challenge. Real GDP grew by 75 percent from 1940 to 1945. Industry had the ability to produce far more than most people had ever imagined; all it needed was a customer with the means to pay.

As the war ended, government officials and policymakers had to figure out what to do with this new industrial capacity. Should the country simply close down the new factories and return to the level of output and unemployment that it had in 1940? Or should it convert the capacity to peacetime use, and come up with new sources of demand to replace government arms spending? This question marked a subtle shift from Keynesianism as a method of moderating business cycles to Keynesianism as a strategy for economic growth, with a whole cohort of postwar policymakers embracing the Keynesian idea that the key to avoiding mass unemployment was to ensure sufficient aggregate demand. As Robert Nathan, chair of the War Production Board's Planning Committee, put it, "If increased buying power can be gotten into the hands of consumers who will spend it for goods and services, American industry need not worry about finding markets for all it can produce, and produce profitably."

Imbued with the patriotism and solidarity of the era, many officials felt it was their responsibility to reflect on these lessons and share them with their fellow Americans. Indeed, Bowles was not the only one explaining this vision for a new economic future. Nathan wrote his own book, *Mobilizing for Abundance* (1944), to explain how Keynesian economics could bring widespread prosperity after the war, as did journalist and future senator Blair Moody in *Boom or Bust* (1941) and Vice President Henry Wallace in *Sixty Million Jobs* (1945). Indeed, so invested were everyday Americans in restoring and contributing to the overall economy that when the Pabst Brewing Company sponsored a contest to come up with plans for postwar employment, it received nearly 36,000 entries.

Americans understood the stakes of the transition to peacetime. The connection between economic turmoil and political conflict was clear to those who had watched the rise of fascism in the 1920s and '30s. The development of atomic weapons meant that a third world war would almost certainly end civilization while, at the same time, the experience of war production offered the prospect of boundless opportunities and prosperity. This stark trade-off—civilizational annihilation on one hand, endless prosperity on the other—made it extremely important to get the transition right. And it was clear that doing so was only possible if the American people were brought fully on board.

Bowles grasped the importance of this communications role as deeply as anyone. He had made his first career in advertising, and his firm, Benton and Bowles, was perhaps the most successful ad agency of the Depression era. (It played a major role in developing the radio soap opera.) Part of his success as director of the Office of Price Administration during the war was his decision to turn it into a mass organization, mobilizing volunteers to distribute ration cards and monitor price levels, and in so doing take ownership of the agency. As his friend Galbraith said of him, "Few men in public life have had greater ability to get a problem into comprehensible form—where F.D.R. paraphrased to make an issue seem understandable, Bowles always kept the real situation in view."

Indeed, in *Tomorrow Without Fear*, Bowles pitched his explanations of Keynesian theory to resonate with Americans' intuitive, shared experience. Contrasting the booming wartime economy with the trepidation in 1940, for example, he asked: "Did we feel insecure in 1940 because we thought we couldn't produce all the goods and services we needed?" The answer, of course, is no, and Bowles goes on to identify this as "the baffling paradox of the times, the inability of people on every hand to find markets for the goods that people on every hand so badly needed!" Bowles's optimism is palpable, and it is an inclusive optimism—from the book's dedication to the men and women of the armed forces to its description of what life ahead might look like for every farmer, worker, and businessman. Throughout the book, Bowles pauses to marvel at the ingenuity of his fellow citizens. "It always surprises me," he begins one chapter, "that a people so proud of their achievements as we Americans often fail to realize how great some of these achievements actually are and how far we have come."

Despite their patriotism and optimism, however, Bowles and his contemporary prophets of abundance were under no illusions about the challenges that widespread prosperity, even if it were secured, would bring. In 1930 Keynes had anticipated the possibility of an end to scarcity in his essay "Economic Possibilities for our Grand-children," speculating about the enormous cultural adjustment it would require. If the "economic problem" of subsistence—"hitherto the primary, most pressing problem of the human race"—was solved, then, Keynes wrote, "I think with dread of the readjustment of the habits and instincts of the ordinary man, bred into him for countless generations, which he may be asked to discard within a few decades . . . must we not expect a general 'nervous breakdown'?" Ever the ad man, Bowles in *Tomorrow Without Fear* translated this "economic problem" into the difficulty of "learning to live better." We know we can produce, he wrote. But what we don't yet know is if we can learn to "use our productive capacity to raise our standards of living, to lighten the burden of toil for all of our people." This learning curve would require a maturation of sorts, and "if we can't grow up with it . . . the very achievements of our science and technology will be our undoing. And what could be more ridiculous!"

LEARNING TO LIVE BETTER was of such concern because a direct implication of Keynesian economic theory is that inequality is in itself harmful for growth. Keynes concluded *The General Theory* by stating, "The outstanding faults of the economic society in which we live are its failure to provide for full employment and its arbitrary and inequitable distribution of wealth and incomes." Other Keynesian thinkers would make the direct link between those two faults: high levels of inequality make unemployment more likely. As Marriner S. Eccles, chairman of the Federal Reserve from 1934 to 1948, put it, "as mass production economy has to be accompanied by mass consumption, mass consumption, in turn, implies a distribution of wealth . . . to provide men with buying power equal to the amount of goods and services offered by the nation's economic machinery." In Bowles's formulation, "the redistribution of income is a subject which many people find distasteful to talk about—much less to do something about. But talk about it and do something about it we must, because this is not a matter of taste; it is a matter of national economic necessity."

The key point is that businesses will only produce when there is demand for their products, otherwise they will shutter their facilities and lay off their workers. Because high-income people spend a smaller share of their earnings than low-income people do, high levels of income inequality result in lower levels of aggregate demand, the forerunner to recession and unemployment. Bowles demonstrated this logic by taking it to its extreme:

> Let us suppose that one percent of the population were to receive 95 percent of our entire national income, with the remaining 5 percent spread among the rest of us. Could our system—could any system—work on that basis? One percent of the people couldn't possibly consume 95 percent of all the goods and services which the rest of us could produce.

The long-lasting prosperity of the 1940s and '50s thus owed, in large part, to the fact that the general public broadly understood and agreed upon the economic principle that fast-paced growth and high employment could be achieved on the back of consumer demand, but only if purchasing power was distributed widely enough.

Once armed with this information, the general public went about enforcing it. As Lizabeth Cohen documents in *A Consumer's Republic* (2003), labor unions cited the importance of maintaining high demand through widely distributed purchasing power to justify their calls for higher wages. As George Meany, secretary-treasurer of the AFL, put it in 1944, "we have the machinery to build all of the automobiles, all of the radios, washing machines and such things; we have the workers to build all of the houses that we could possibly use. But we will not make those things unless there is purchasing power available to buy them."

Across the negotiating table, business executives also acknowledged the need for mass consumer purchasing power. During the final years of World War II, the head of research for the magazine publisher McFadden told his audience of advertisers, "As every manufacturer knows . . . there can be no high levels of production and employment unless the products of industry are bought by the workers." Henry Ford used the same logic when he decided to pay his workers enough to buy the cars they made. Keeping wages low is penny wise, pound foolish.

Demand-side growth also had bipartisan support. President Harry Truman, a Democrat, made it a cornerstone of his economic policy and appointed pro-growth economist Leon Keyserling to lead the newly created Council of Economic Advisers. Ten years later, President Dwight Eisenhower, a Republican, supported the expansion of benefits for seniors as a means of boosting demand and getting the country out of the 1958 recession.

This era is commonly remembered as the Golden Age of Capitalism, and for good reason: the results of this consensus on demand-driven growth are hard to dispute. Productive capacity and living standards grew in lockstep for twenty-five years, at rates never yet equaled. This equitably distributed growth meant that children who lived through this era had a greater than 80 percent chance of outearning their parents as adults. Among today's young adults, the rate is just 50 percent.

WHAT HAPPENED? Keynesian economics fell out of favor for a variety of reasons, from reluctant business executives who didn't want to lose leverage over their employees to classical laissez-faire economists in the 1970s who used the stagflation crisis to reassert the Victorian belief that government should not intervene in markets. This was the state of mainstream economics in 2007 when the Great Recession hit. That crisis brought about a "Return of Keynes" just in time to keep the economy from fully collapsing, and in 2008, even Robert Lucas—the developer of the rational expectations hypothesis that did much to undo Keynesianism—admitted that "everyone is a Keynesian in a foxhole."

Just as Keynes's star is rising once again among academics, Bowles's example of communicating the Keynesian vision in terms that people can understand—and care about—is starting to catch on in economics education. At Washington University in St. Louis, Steven Fazzari has developed an introduction to "Muddy Water" macroeconomics, explaining Keynes's theories—and those of his critics—in accessible language. At Harvard, Raj Chetty is teaching an economics based on empirical data, rather than parsimonious models. And most promising of all, a group of economists—which includes none other than Samuel Bowles, Chester Bowles's son—has created the CORE Econ project, an attempt to totally reinvent introductory economics, starting with the textbook itself. Where standard introductory economics textbooks cost upward of a hundred dollars a copy (the Harvard economist N. Gregory Mankiw, author of the widely used textbook *Principles of Economics*, has made as much as $42 million in royalties since the first edition was released in 1997), CORE's *The Economy* is available online for free. And where standard courses often begin with an abstract discussion of supply and demand, CORE is grounded in directly addressing contemporary challenges: income inequality is the subject of its textbook's first chapter.

Yet while Keynesian thinking is beginning to resurface in the academy, it still has a long way to go in terms of shaping popular and policy discourse. This is true even though Keynesian analysis seems singularly well suited to current troubles. Today we have almost unprecedented levels of income inequality combined with sustained low growth. We are still digging our way out from a massive economic slump whose root and proximate causes have remarkable parallels with those that animated Keynes. All of the ingredients that went into *The General Theory* and that showed the shortcomings of classical economics are present today as well.

This will be even more true going forward. Consider the case of automation, which many people fear will cause unemployment; Andrew Yang is running a whole presidential campaign on it. But as many have noted, it is not the robots themselves that we have to fear, but the continued decline of worker bargaining power. If incomes can be made to rise alongside automation—whether through higher wages, a shorter work week, or a universal basic income—we don't have anything to fear from robots. In fact, this is the world that Keynes dreamed of in "Economic Possibilities for Our Grandchildren." The reason we have come up short is not our technology but our political economy.

Keynesian economics offers the opportunity to connect the two largest economic problems of our time—slow growth and extreme inequality—with a compelling theory that the latter causes the former. After all, large numbers of businesses today are struggling because their core consumers no longer have the money to buy their products. Even wealthy investors are struggling with what the business press calls "capital superabundance." There is far more money to invest than there are promising investment opportunities, which keeps returns down. At its most fundamental level, this problem is a shortfall of demand: just as in the 1930s, the capital exists to produce far more than we currently do, if only the people who need things had the money to buy them.

To a Keynesian, the way to revive and stabilize economic growth is to increase the purchasing power of low- and middle-income consumers. A Keynesian growth program would thus allow room for some traditionally conservative constituencies to get on board with progressive policies such as child allowances, a job guarantee, and a fifteen dollar minimum wage. Far from being a drain on the economy, these policies are our tickets out of secular stagnation.

Keynesian economics also carries a positive moral message. Unlike the "Greed is good" mantra of the 1980s, Keynesian analysis argues that selfishness leads to ruin and that you should help your neighbor. Bowles makes this point well in *Tomorrow Without Fear*:

> In our modern world, for the first time in history, what makes good morals makes good economics, too. As we organize our economy to provide more and better food for the hungry, the corner grocer and the

farmer find their incomes increased. . . . Greater equity in sharing our economic pie costs no one anything. Instead it means a bigger pie for all of us to share and, hence, more pie for every one of us.

While it is dramatic in its ambitions, the Keynesian approach is far from a risk: no other strategy has been tested so thoroughly and with such great success. As Bowles understood, the key is to communicate it.

EVERYDAY ECONOMISTS
Samuel Bowles interviewed by Joshua Cohen

HOW DO WE TALK about economics? Robert Manduca's essay "Selling Keynesianism" notes a striking connection between the concerns about public education that led Chester Bowles to write *Tomorrow Without Fear* in 1946 and those that led his son Samuel Bowles to develop the Curriculum Open-Access Resources in Economics (CORE) Project, an innovative economics curriculum for undergraduates. Bowles is a distinguished economist and longtime *Boston Review* contributor. In this discussion with *Boston Review* editor Joshua Cohen, Bowles reflects on his father's work, the connections with his own efforts, and the need for new ways to communicate economics today.

JOSHUA COHEN: I want to talk with you today about economics—both the discipline and efforts to communicate and educate about the discipline. And I want to start with your father, Chester Bowles. He was born in 1901, graduated from Yale in 1924, and started the advertising firm of Benton and Bowles, which was incredibly successful even during the Great Depression. Then during World War II, he ran the Office of Price Administration, working on price and rent controls. After the war, he was governor of Connecticut, ambassador to India (on two different occasions), and was elected to the House of Representatives in 1958. But of his many accomplishments, the one I want to talk about today is a book he wrote in 1946 called *Tomorrow Without Fear.* The book is an amazing effort to communicate economic principles to the public. By way of introduction, I want to share a quote from economist John Kenneth Galbraith. In the *New York Times* in 1971, Galbraith wrote that your father, who was his friend, possessed "an almost unlimited faith in the possibilities of public persuasion. No one, in his view, is so benighted that he is beyond reach of a convincing memorandum or a good long, persuasive talk. . . . Few men in public life have had greater ability to get a problem into comprehensible form." That's an extraordinary statement, and it is absolutely true that *Tomorrow Without Fear* is an effort at public communication that reads like a good, persuasive talk. The book is now available online due to the good work of issue contributor Robert Manduca. But as an economist yourself, I want to get your view of *Tomorrow Without Fear.*

SAMUEL BOWLES: Well, I first read the book more than a half century ago, and I reread it recently now that it's available online. And there are many things about the work that I find really remarkable on a second reading.

One thing that is striking is how the book reflects what he learned as a former ad man, even though he hated advertising and was very happy to get out of it. He never had a good word to say about it when I was growing up, but he learned two important things during that time in the 1930s. The first is that you can't sell vacuum cleaners to households that don't have any money—no amount of advertising is going to solve that problem. He spoke poignantly about going door to door to figure out what was wrong with their advertising campaign and being told over and over again, "I'd be very happy to buy your machine if my husband had a job." So, he understood the problem of aggregate demand in the economy, although he never would have used that term.

The second thing he learned from the advertising industry is, of course, the absolute importance of communication.

So at the end of World War II, when the United States was facing a problem of inadequate spending and might again return to depression, he sat down to write *Tomorrow Without Fear*. There's the sense in those pages of the urgency and danger of the time. As he put it, "I want to see, if possible, what economic lessons there are for us in the greatest of all depressions and the greatest of all wars." That's how he approached this key idea that if ordinary people didn't have enough money, the economy couldn't prosper.

jc: I find it striking that the book is a popular exposition of Keynesian ideas but never actually mentions John Maynard Keynes.

sb: The fact that Keynes is not there is not surprising to me. My father never argued from authority. He never quoted this source or that source. For facts he would, but he always wanted to give you the commonsense explanation of why something worked. He was perhaps a bit anti-academic. I heard lots of epithets and unpleasant words for intellectuals around the dinner table, starting with "egghead" but getting much worse. So, when I ended up becoming an academic, my dad asked me more than once to please go back to his friend (and my former teacher) Galbraith and see what advice I could get on how to advance public understanding about economics.

But there's something else in the book that is not from Keynesian economics: the importance of government and collective action. Based on his wartime experience heading the OPA and seeing the coming together of the entire nation, he was convinced that, if we could only work together during peacetime as well as we had during the war, then we could really succeed on a grand scale. So the book was propelled by the war and depression, which clearly established the problems (full employment and shared prosperity)—combined with an immense confidence in collective action through trade unions, business associations, and, importantly, the federal government.

I've recently been reading a contemporary textbook, Paul Samuelson's *Economics: An Introductory Analysis*. It was the first really big introduction to economics and was published two years after my dad's little pamphlet. It expressed the same mixture of danger and confidence. The very first question for students to discuss in Samuelson's textbook was: "How do you expect to fare in the next depression?" That was the sense of the times, and I think we often forget today what a dangerous time it was.

And the confidence was not entirely misplaced. The radical break with the old economics by Samuelson—who made Keynesian economics an essential part of what all economists and many citizens would know—and the efforts of people such as my dad communicating related ideas to a broader public, changed how we talked about the economy. Along with a new vernacular came a set of policies that for about thirty years following World War II, brought us what is now called the Golden Age of Capitalism. During this period, things turned out more or less as my dad had hoped. Not quite, of course, but wages rose a little faster even than productivity, Samuelson's "next great depression" did not materialize, and the global capitalist economy grew at unprecedented rates. Having contributed to this was a fantastic accomplishment of this generation of public servants and intellectuals.

JC: And it was very different from the public sensibility now. *Tomorrow Without Fear* emphasizes the importance of demand, so that the heroes of the book are consumers, not the vaunted job creators we hear about today. And if you're going to get a lot of demand in the economy, you have to be concerned with the distribution of income, so there's a lot of discussion about ideal income distribution. In fact, he describes what the distribution of income in the 1960s might look like if things go well: the bottom third of the population should earn 17 percent of national income. Well, right now, the bottom 50 percent get 12.5 percent, so we're far today from where your father wanted us to be.

I'd like to come back to what you said about how your father wanted to address the concerns that people had about their lives.

There's a paragraph on the first page where he's describing his experience during the war at the Office of Price Administration and the *millions* of phone calls and letters his office would get each week from people all over the country. He says, "almost always these people, in addition to their specific problems, have raised general questions that open the door on tomorrow."

So, the book, in a very literal way, is responding to the questions people had about future prosperity. This is not some imaginary dialogue. And if you reflect on the fact that this was a world before the Internet and email, the sheer volume of communication he was receiving is extraordinary. It's an interesting view both of democracy and of him as a public servant.

SB: Yes, he was very moved by those conversations, and when I was a young boy, they were repeated to me long after they had taken place. Of course, these people were worried about their own situation, but they were always presented as if the person was also seeking solutions to larger problems. Implicit was a kind of civic-mindedness that he took for granted in most people.

As an empirical matter, that was probably true of some and not true of others, but the key idea my dad had was that it doesn't have to be warfare that promotes public service and civic-mindedness. And I think he saw a number of other situations as his life progressed—the civil rights movement, the anti–Vietnam War movement—that confirmed for him that nations could be moved to action on grounds other than narrow national or individual interest.

One of the things that I found particularly striking early in the book was that he had a very inclusive idea of "we." "Economic security," he wrote, "based on abundant production, fairly shared, is our goal whether we live on the Rue Saint Jacques or on Main Street, U.S.A., whether we farm in a giant collective in the Ukraine or till the black soil of Iowa." I was shocked when I read that he was including the people of the Soviet Union in his discussion about what it is that "we" all want! This is 1946, before the Cold War was in high gear, but the inclusiveness of all of these different possible approaches was striking to me—the internationalism of it and the breadth of it.

JC: I want to jump forward to work you are doing now. One of the things I was immediately struck by when I read *Tomorrow Without Fear* was how its role in public communicating about economics connects to CORE, which you initiated along with Wendy Carlin and others. CORE is all about reimagining and reconfiguring economics education for undergraduates. How did you come to that work?

SB: CORE is a response to the economic and financial crisis of 2008 and to the growing concerns about economic injustice and climate change. About a dozen or so of us who were involved in getting the project off the ground had a sense that these problems had to be addressed. We had a sense similar to the danger and foreboding that my father and Samuelson had felt after World War II. But also a sense of the possibilities. We were also convinced, as they were, that economics had recently changed in such a way that it could address some of these problems more adequately than it had in the past. Our mission and our confidence grew from a combination of a new set of problems that we saw looming and the changes in economics that had been accumulating over the past thirty years.

In a sense we also started like my dad had, with a set of questions from non-economists. We asked students around the world—at twenty-five different universities—what questions they thought economists should be addressing today. These students had never studied economics before, and we asked them to just write their response down on a piece of paper in one or two words. Then we made word clouds from the responses, and the results were striking. The word "inequality" was huge. Next was "climate change" and related terms, and "instability" and "robots" were a bit further down. It didn't matter where in the world we did this, we got the same word clouds. It also didn't matter if we did this with students or—and I know this sounds odd, but it's true—bankers. Carlin and I did the same thing with 120 professionals at the central bank and at New Zealand's treasury, and we got almost the exact same thing as we got with students.

People today think that economics should be addressing inequality, climate change, instability, the future of work, and innovation. But none of these issues play any substantial role in what our introductory economics students are learning. So, we decided that the usual rule of textbook writing—which is that you can only change 15 percent of content when you write a new book—would have to be thrown to the winds. In the same way that Samuelson turned his textbook upside down—he began with macroeconomics, which was a radical change—we began our book with questions of innovation, wealth creation, inequality, and climate change.

About his book, Samuelson wrote something along the lines of, "What I've written here is what every economist under the age of fifty already knows and has been using in his research for the past decade." I think that CORE could say the same. Most of what we have included is familiar to recently trained graduate students, but not included in the introductory courses. Or, if they are, they are tacked on at the end, in chapters that are never assigned.

We also felt strongly that digitized knowledge that can be made available to additional users at zero expense should not cost students hundreds of dollars. So, we put together a model to make that work, and the curriculum is now available for free online.

JC: There is a difference between CORE as I understand it and the project of *Tomorrow Without Fear*. Your father begins his book by commenting that he is not an academic or economist, but an American anxious to contribute solutions to his country's problems. And then he addresses the public in his pamphlet. CORE, on the other hand, is a textbook used in universities. How do you think about those different acts of communication and is there an element of CORE that aims to reach outside the university setting?

SB: The analogy that I would offer very immodestly would be with Samuelson's textbook and not with my father's pamphlet. But CORE and my father's pamphlet share something in common, which is that both are interested in providing a new way of explaining the economy to people who were not intending to go on in economics. The pamphlet might have been the only thing that a person ever read on economics, and this course might be the only one a student ever takes in economics. That part is very consistent.

But my father's pamphlet was a hundred pages. CORE is over a thousand pages. So we're a bit more ambitious. My father was trying to convince people that a set of public policies could be implemented —and many of them were. CORE does not advocate for particular policies. What we're advocating for is a new way of understanding how the economy works, what people are like, how we interact in the economy, and how we interact with our biosphere. In a sense, we're trying to provide people with a framework which will allow them to participate in debates on public policy; we're training people's capacities to form their own ideas. And I think that is an essential part in changing the way economics is done and changing the way economic policy is made.

There is another theme common to CORE and to *Tomorrow Without Fear*: they both challenge the idea that any economy can function well if people are—or are assumed to be—entirely self-interested and amoral. My dad wrote: "it has always been true that those communities in which the strong extended a helping hand to their weaker neighbors have been economically stronger and healthier for it. But only in recent generations has it become true that the smooth functioning of our economy . . . actually requires the practice of the best of our moral teachings." True then and truer now. No combination of greed, fear, and clever contracts can make a modern economy—based on knowledge production and distribution, and caring for others—work well even in the short run, much less provide the basis for a sustainable future of our biosphere.

If you talk to people like foundation presidents, they're constantly going on about getting the "right people" in the room so they can figure out the right solutions to this problem and that problem. They are not talking about a very large room. This is not the CORE approach. Yes, of course, we need good ideas, and thanks to groups such as Economics for Inclusive Prosperity we will have plenty. But we also need a public that is economically articulate in demanding policies that are consistent with a democratic and fair society. That's what I think an economics program like CORE or like Samuelson's book or like my dad's pamphlet are all trying to do—all in their slightly different ways.

JC: It's very hard for me to think of anything similar to *Tomorrow Without Fear* today. Where could someone who is not a university student turn to get that kind of extremely thoughtful, practically oriented picture of what the economic problems of the country are and what might be done about them?

SB: That is very true. There is nothing like *Tomorrow Without Fear* for today. I would say that the conservative position was greatly bolstered by Milton Friedman's *Capitalism and Freedom* (1962) because it expressed a particular view of how the economy worked, it was beautifully written, and it was argued by a very serious intellectual who promoted interesting ideas such as the negative income tax and school vouchers. It had a normative framework—a limited view of freedom—and it had a few policies that were emblematic of that framework. It seems to me that something like that is exactly what we need today.

I think people are quite convinced that the way charted by Friedman will not work and, in fact, is part of the problems we now confront. But I don't think we yet have a statement in everyday language that seriously argues for a reconstruction of political economy—both normatively and analytically. I do think it can be done because the groundwork is there. That is a book waiting to be written.

jc: We have our marching orders then.

WHO OWNS CORPORATIONS?
Lenore Palladino

IN 1962 MILTON FRIEDMAN—the economist who, more than anyone else, worked to undo Keynesian theory—published his landmark book, *Capitalism and Freedom*. In it, he argued for many of the policies we now call libertarian or neoliberal: free markets promote freedom, government intervention does not, and therefore government should be extremely limited. But the book was also crucial in advancing what is now known as the theory of shareholder primacy, the idea that corporations have no higher purpose than maximizing profits for their shareholders. "Few trends," Friedman wrote, "could so thoroughly undermine the very foundation of our free society as the acceptance by corporate officials of a social responsibility other than to make as much money for their stockholders as possible."

By 1970 he was expanding on this theory even more. Since markets are efficient, he argued, corporations should be constituted like markets; and since shareholders are the only stakeholders in the company who assume risk, the corporation's purpose should be to generate returns for them. The messy and complex power dynamics of group interactions were thus written out of the story, and decision-making within corporations, Friedman and his acolytes argued, should focus on a singular goal, an "optimum": maximizing shareholder value. "The key point," he wrote in an essay for the *New York Times Magazine*, "is that, in his capacity as a corporate executive, the manager is the agent of the individuals who own the corporation . . . and his primary responsibility is to them."

For the past fifty years, virtually all business leaders, many policymakers, and a great deal of voters have accepted Friedman's argument that shareholder primacy is the "natural" law of the market. Yet the shareholder-focused corporation is not a law of nature, nor does that governance model accurately reflect today's business dealings. This misguided focus is the result of decades of flawed theory in economics and law. It stems from an incorrect analysis of the relationships between shareholders, employees, management, and the corporation itself. And it is based on a flawed theory of the underlying economy: that markets work perfectly, and the heavy hand of government must get out of the way.

This ideology has caused immeasurable harm. The singular focus on stock price means that wealth is extracted by a small number of shareholders while those who work to produce that wealth are squeezed to the bone. Large corporations operating in this way so dominate U.S. political, economic, and social life that it is difficult for most of us to remember that the rules that shape corporate governance are democratically determined—that we, the electorate, can actually change them.

Who owns a corporation, after all? Friedman referred to the shareholders as the owners. According to this way of thinking, a business corporation is nothing but a collection of shares, so whoever owns the shares owns the corporation—and thus should be able to decide how to govern it.

In reality, however—as well as in law—corporations own themselves. Corporations are legal entities that require state government approval. Once incorporated, they have tremendous privileges to operate apart from the people who form them and run them: they have perpetual existence, limited liability, and the ability to take out debt in their own name. Corporations are different from other forms of businesses, such as sole proprietorships or LLCs, where there is no formal legal separation between the founders that profit from and run a business and the business itself. The very purpose of incorporating a business is to create an entity that lives on its own; it exists in perpetuity and is not just an extension of those who provide its capital.

Despite this fundamental separation, the delusion that shareholders are the exclusive owners of business corporations in the United States has persisted, causing most corporations to then govern themselves by the theory of shareholder primacy. But it does not have to be this way. New policies could ensure that all the stakeholders who collectively generate a corporation's prosperity then benefit from its wealth.

Corporations have multiple stakeholders other than shareholders, including employees, customers, suppliers, and communities. In this essay, I will focus on one set of stakeholders—employees—because changes to corporate law to include employees as equals in corporate ownership and governance would be radically pragmatic. Employees could hold corporate equity shares in an employee ownership trust to more equitably distribute a corporation's wealth. And employees could serve on corporate boards of directors alongside shareholders and management to ensure the corporation is governed both by those who take risks on its behalf and those who are affected most directly by its decisions.

These reforms, which should also include a new articulation of a corporation's purpose and a change to corporate "fiduciary duty," require procedural changes in how incorporation happens in the United States. The goal is not to predetermine certain business outcomes—say, a set wage for workers or a set percentage of profits reinvested in the corporations—but to fundamentally rebalance power among three of the most important corporate stakeholders: employees, shareholders, and management. These changes would not automatically solve today's economic problems, but they would stop us from hurtling down the path we are on, a path that sacrifices worker and community well-being at the altar of shareholder wealth maximization.

THE IDEA THAT SHAREHOLDERS are the true "owners" of corporations dates back to Adolf Berle and Gardiner Means's *The Modern Corporation* (1932). Their conclusion, which is still the touchstone for theorists of corporate governance, was that the shareholder is like the captain at sea: others (i.e., management) plotted the course and steered the ship, but the captain put up the capital and knew why the ship was setting off and where it was going. In their words, the direction or purpose of the vessel was set by and could only be altered "by the persons having the underlying property interest."

If shareholders are seen as the true owners of corporations, then the management must be forced, through carrot or stick, to maximize value for shareholders. Otherwise there is potential for managers to use corporate funds for their own personal benefit. The only way to solve "the separation of ownership from control" was to revest control in the hands of shareholders.

Despite Berle and Means's theory, however, early and mid-twentieth-century America was dominated by "managerialist" corporations such as General Electric and General Motors. These large conglomerates had strong managers who prioritized stable growth and who bargained with powerful unions. Shareholders were passive, receiving steady dividends but exerting little authority within the firm.

Shareholder primacy as an economic and legal theory took off in the 1970s. Against the backdrop of economic stagnation and the rise of neoliberalism, economists such as Friedman focused on the notion that corporations are just another kind of efficient market. The business corporation was thus seen as a collection of financial assets, and management was expected to have a financial background as opposed to an industrial background. Economists justified why shareholders should expect managers to squeeze as much value out of the firm for them as possible and argued that shareholders should no longer be content with steady dividends but should reassert their role as "principals" who need to discipline the "agent" managers.

Palladino

Academic economists built upon and formalized Friedman's arguments throughout the 1970s, forming what continues to be the mainstream economic analysis of the corporation today. Crucially, much of this analysis moved beyond the earlier idea from Berle and Means that shareholders were owners. Shareholders no longer exercised the responsibilities that usually accompany ownership rights, so instead, this new cohort of economists extended Friedman's claims about market efficiency to the specific institution of the corporation and argued that a corporation is nothing but a "nexus of contracts." In other words, the firm is not an independent organization but rather a marketplace where different contracts are freely made. As Armen Alchian and Harold Demsetz put it in 1972, "the firm . . . has no power of fiat, no authority, no disciplinary action any different in the slightest degree from ordinary market contracting between two people."

This conception led to the key argument in favor of shareholder primacy: shareholders have a distinctive relationship to the corporation. All other stakeholders have "complete contracts"—employment contracts or contracts for a fixed return on a bond. Shareholders, in contrast, have an incomplete contractual relationship with the corporation because no dividend or capital gains are guaranteed. Since they do not have a fixed contract, shareholders must have control rights or else they will not put capital into the corporation.

The corporation was thus bleached of organizational politics and power. The move replaced the corporation as a site of contribution by many stakeholders—where contributions of and gains to each group are subject to disagreement, negotiation, and power struggles—with a market-based view. Turning the corporation into a kind of market means, as Michael C. Jensen and William H. Meckling wrote in 1976, that "conflicting objectives of individuals are brought into equilibrium within a framework of contractual relations." In other words, if corporations are just a nexus of contracts, then all relations among corporate stakeholders are determined purely and efficiently by market forces, and their interests are "protected by contractual and regulatory means rather than through participation in corporate governance." Notably, employees should be content with the wage determined for them by the invisible hand of the market.

Moreover, because shareholder interests are primary, shareholders should govern the corporation in order to discipline management into serving their interests. This conclusion, called "agency theory," holds that agents (managers) do not automatically do what the principal wants. A manager may be content to let wages rise to avoid strife in the workplace, since his financial remuneration is not affected by higher costs. What matters to managers is only their share in the wealth reduction—not all of the wealth lost. It is the shareholders who lose out as employee costs rise which is why shareholders must monitor managers' behavior and induce them through various mechanisms (sufficient motivation or fear of repercussion) to align their interests with that of their principals.

NEGLECTING ORGANIZATIONAL REALITIES, however, leads shareholder primacy into two major mistakes: it ignores how corporations produce and innovate, and it sees shareholders as the sole risk-takers when, in fact, they are often protected and very removed.

First, as William Lazonick's *Theory of the Innovative Enterprise* (2013) explains, shareholder primacy lacks a theory for how corporations actually develop new ideas for products, new marketing strategies, and new means of using resources. Innovation depends on financial resources, but it crucially also involves "strategic control and organizational integration" in social conditions that are "uncertain, collective and cumulative" in character. Put simply, successful corporations are human organizations that depend on the risky, long-term, creative collaboration of different kinds of participants. This is obvious to anyone in the business world but absent from a "nexus of contracts" view of the corporation. Investors buying and selling shares with each other in diversified portfolios are not walking the shop floor. They are not surveying customers to iterate successful products or competing with coworkers for the highest sales.

The second mistake is to see shareholders as the sole risk-takers, or even to see them as contributing to the corporation directly at all. When Berle and Means wrote their book, the bulk of corporate growth came from new issuances of stock, which, they said, kept management accountable to suppliers of capital since they depended on capital for future growth. But none of this makes any sense in current capital markets.

Most shareholders today, after all, are *traders*, not initial investors in a company's initial public offering (IPO). These traders—all of us holding corporate stock in a retirement portfolio, for example—do not think of themselves as "owners" since they are not contributing directly to the corporation's capital. The fact that our ownership is mediated through a very long chain of financial investors, whose interest is often to earn fees through trading volume rather than sustainable growth of corporate wealth, means that retail shareholders are even further cut off from business decisions.

Today there are only two types of shareholders with real power. First, minority shareholder "activists," who have leveraged the massive holdings of institutional investors to exercise actual power over boards and corporations. And, second, the private equity funds that take over companies to extract wealth regardless of the impact on future productivity—the opposite of what an owner is supposed to do. Notwithstanding these two groups, retail shareholders—you and I invested through our 401(k)s or mutual funds—do not actually exercise control over corporations.

Moreover, the claim that shareholders assume the most risk lumps together diversifiable and undiversifiable risk. Shareholders of large public corporations today are not generally taking a risk on the profitability of a given firm. Instead, they are diversified investors who scarcely notice the particular rising or falling share price of a given company, because they have reduced their risk by holding a broad cross section of the market. Of course, they still take a risk that the entire market will fall (as happened in 2009) and that they will not be able to sell their investment when they need to. But concluding that their risk is different in kind from the risk an employee or bondholder takes no longer makes sense. As even Berle and Means noted, security holders "may be regarded as a hierarchy of individuals, all of whom have supplied capital to the enterprise, and all of whom expect return from it."

Workers, by contrast, contribute more to creating corporate wealth and long-term productivity than a person whose share has already been traded 10 or 10,000 times. And their deep investment in the corporation is not diversified—their risk and rewards depend entirely on the profitability of the corporation. If a corporation's profits plunge and layoffs follow, workers face the tremendous hurdles of finding new employment, relocating, or collecting scant unemployment.

THE CURRENT MODEL of shareholder primacy is simply not a reflection of today's reality. It treats labor as a cost to be contained while a true reckoning with how corporations operate reveals the significant risks that workers take on as well as their contributions to organizational success. Transitioning to a stakeholder model for corporations—specifically, employee governance and employee ownership funds—makes better sense of employee contributions while also mitigating some of the worst outcomes of the obsession with a constantly rising share price.

I referred earlier to implementation of the employee governance model as "radically pragmatic" because some straightforward, politically obvious changes could have a huge effect on economic inequality. In the United States, corporate law is state law: incorporation is accomplished at the state level, and the "internal affairs doctrine" allows corporations to choose a state for incorporation that is not otherwise tied to their business activities and to have their corporate internal affairs governed by that state's rules. Practically, this has meant that Delaware has become the state of choice for large corporations, due to its historical offerings of business-friendly corporate law. Reforming corporate law at the state level would thus be politically very difficult since it would all unravel if one state sticks with shareholder primacy.

Three federal reforms would get around this hurdle. First, and most crucially, Congress can mandate that large corporations (say, those over $1 billion in annual revenue) be required to charter federally. This change—as proposed in Elizabeth Warren's Accountable Capitalism Act—would ensure the remaining reforms would be enacted, including number two: a redefinition of "fiduciary duties." By redefining a board's fiduciary duties to include more than just shareholders, the board of directors would be accountable to more stakeholders. This change might seem weak since it would not prescribe a certain outcome for the various stakeholders, nor would it specify how boards should balance the different interests of stakeholders. Still, it would make the decision to pay out billions in stock buybacks while firing employees a lot more difficult for boards to justify. Currently, corporate boards engage in this behavior and then hide behind the excuse that their only responsibility is to shareholders.

More positively, this reform would encourage corporations to form boards made up of individuals from multiple stakeholder groups—including employees—in order to weigh the impacts of major corporate decisions on all groups at the table. The board is the ultimate decision-making authority, after all: hiring and firing the chief executive, making major financial decisions, and bearing legal responsibility for the affairs of the corporation. Employees should have a say in these matters. Proposals vary about how best to include employees on boards, but it should be obvious that "token" employee representation is not sufficient: the point is to ensure that employees have a meaningful voice in corporate decisions. This is crucial since courts adjudicate board decisions using the business judgment rule—meaning that, in the absence of fraud or malfeasance, judges do not rule on the substance of decisions, they simply look to see if the board followed proper procedures. In other words, if fiduciary duty were redefined, boards would have to show evidence that they had taken the interests of multiple groups of stakeholders into account.

Finally, corporate purpose statements, which are filed as part of the charter at the time of incorporation, should include a requirement of positive social benefit. Benefit corporations such as Patagonia and Kickstarter already adhere to this standard, vowing to create "general public benefit," which is defined as a "material positive impact on society and the environment, taken as a whole." Currently, corporate purpose statements simply require that companies stay within the bounds of the law. If implemented, the public benefit standard would be incredibly difficult to judge at such a high level of abstraction, but it could be a way to force companies to reckon with egregious pollution or community harm.

ONCE WE CHANGE corporate governance to be more democratic and reflective of the realities of contributions and risks, the other major area for policy reform is to grant employees shares of corporate equity in a collective trust, or "employee ownership."

At its most basic level, employee ownership creates a right to a share of the profits when businesses do well. Less tangibly, employee ownership also gives workers the ability to vote for the company's board of directors and other major decisions that the company's external shareholders traditionally make. Holding equity in an employee trust means that employees are automatically granted their share when they start working for a corporation—they are not risking their own funds to buy shares as an individual.

This would make corporate ownership and governance far more reflective of society. In 2018 the top 10 percent of households owned 86.5 percent of corporate equities, while the bottom 50 percent owned 0.8 percent. New data from the Federal Reserve's Distributional Financial Accounts shows that the trend has gotten steadily worse for the last thirty years. The rates of black and Latinx families owning significant shares has been 30 percent lower than white families for decades. In a company such as Walmart, a few lucky descendants of Sam Walton own over half of the company's shares. Including workers in ownership and governance is necessary to lessen the hold on corporate wealth by affluent white families.

Decades of neoliberal thinking have obfuscated the basic logic that all those who contribute to the success of a corporation should see just rewards. There are signs, however, that this logic is changing. In September 2018, the UK Labour Party proposed a policy for "Inclusive Ownership Funds," which would require corporations with over 250 employees to ensure that employees receive dividends.

The Labour Party's plan is detailed. It ensures that investors are not injured by having their share value diluted because it institutes a transition process: every year, employees gain a 1 percent ownership stake, up to a cap of 10 percent. Once funds are in a trust, then the shares are not available to be resold. This is crucial: the stakes are not a private, freely transferable wealth asset, and since employees don't purchase stakes, they can't sell them when they leave employment. Rather, by becoming an employee of the corporation, you receive an ownership stake in the employee collective trust—a stake that remains in the trust if you move to a different job. So long as you are an employee, though, that stake grants you governance rights and the right to receive a share of the profits.

The proposal has reignited energy in the United States around shared ownership of large corporations. The presidential campaigns of Bernie Sanders, Elizabeth Warren, and Kirsten Gillibrand, for example, have all supported versions of the idea. And employee ownership, in a variety of forms, is broader in the United States than many might think. In knowledge economy sectors where start-ups are common, many companies incentivize employees to join a fledgling start-up with the promise of a big payout down the road, granting equity rather than cash to start. In manufacturing and some service sectors, ownership is more commonly found in the form of a retirement plan, called an ESOP, in which employees are granted stock that is held in trust, and which functions as a form of retirement savings. There is also a growing movement of worker cooperatives and employee-owned businesses among small and medium-sized businesses.

But broad-based employee ownership, meaning share ownership beyond the top executives, is concentrated in certain sectors and certain kinds of plans—the majority of which do not cover the large portion of the U.S. workforce that labors at or near minimum wage. Hospital orderlies, fast-food workers, retail clerks—these workers generally only get a paycheck, and they have not seen a real pay raise in decades. Moreover, because workers of color are concentrated in lower-paid employment, they are less likely to have income to purchase shares on their own.

If we want to transform the inequalities at the heart of our economy, we must address the corporations where the majority of Americans work. Less than 1 percent of U.S. businesses employ over 50 percent of the workforce. These are the most profitable corporations, as well—and, unsurprisingly, the ones that prioritize payments to their shareholders over increasing the wages of their workforce. Meanwhile, CEO "equity-based compensation"—which links CEO compensation to shareholder value—has risen dramatically as a way to ensure management keeps shareholder reward as its north star. In 2017 CEO-to-median worker pay was 312-to-1 and has risen since then as the stock market has climbed.

I would argue that a U.S. "Inclusive Ownership Fund" should be mandatory only for the tiny number of corporations that exert outsize power in the U.S. economy. By my estimate, there are approximately 1,500 corporations with publicly-traded shares that have both an annual revenue over $1 billion and over 1,000 employees. Some of these are household names—such as Walmart or McDonald's —but plenty are the kinds of large corporations that operate in the background of the economy and primarily provide services to other large corporations.

Mandatory employee ownership would also allow these employees to directly engage in the governance of the corporation by participating in the big decisions that determine their futures. Under U.S. law, negotiations between labor unions and corporate management cannot touch on business decisions; instead, discussion is limited to the terms and conditions of employment. This arrangement has locked U.S. workers out of collaborative participation in improving business productivity. By engaging as owners of shares, employees will have the same rights to weigh in as investors do today: in mergers and acquisitions, liquidation, and electing the board of directors.

While some elements of a U.S. plan should differ from the UK version—including the employee threshold for requiring such a plan, or whether some portion of dividends should go to a public fund—the core idea of recognizing workers as stakeholders equal to outside investors bears just as much promise here. It remains the obvious way to rebalance wealth by granting employees a share of the wealth they create, and it could begin the process of reversing decades of wealth extraction by shareholders. We cannot solve economic inequality through wage increases alone: the gaps in wealth are too large.

OF COURSE, corporate boards are not going to share ownership or privileges with employees on their own initiative. Any such change must be driven by public policy. But remember that corporations are creatures of public permission. This means that we—the public—can choose the rules that govern how corporations interact with their stakeholders. Indeed, even Friedman himself saw democratic government playing this role: "government," he wrote in *Capitalism and Freedom*, "is essential both as a forum for determining the 'rules of the game' and as an umpire to interpret and enforce the rules decided on."

Today's rules are broken. Restructuring corporations with employee ownership and governance rights would represent a sharp break from decades of neoliberal policymaking, but we cannot tweak our way out of the mess of deeply-rooted economic inequality. These reforms may not be a silver bullet, but they would ensure the basic standard that employees do well when businesses do well. If corporate executives and shareholders cannot see themselves sharing ownership and governance with employees, perhaps they should try creating value without employees and see how far they get.

THE FALSE PROMISE OF ENLIGHTENMENT
Quinn Slobodian

WE NEED METAPHORS to make sense of reality. But we are often unaware of how those metaphors can then dictate our reality. By defining our problems and challenges, the metaphors we choose to use inadvertently imply solutions. Three recent books, for example, paint a disturbing and dark vision of our present. By their telling, the worlds of data, finance, and law are like aquifers beneath our feet, an alternative geography of accumulation and extraction to which we are each bound by catheter-like lines. Handheld devices transmit our every experience for purposes of revenue creation while the rise and fall of pension funds and asset prices map our futures and those of our children and grandchildren.

If it gives you chills, it is supposed to. All three books are written as conscious interventions into what they see as an unacceptable state of affairs. We need to think carefully about the tales these books tell, but even more carefully about the remedies their metaphors propose. The means of exit or opposition on offer, after all, are conditioned by the symbolic language they use to spook us.

FOR SHOSHANA ZUBOFF, author of *The Age of Surveillance Capitalism* (2019), the status quo is nothing short of pre-apocalyptic. Her book may be the most perfect specimen yet of a genre fated to expand: let us call it the social science horror-memoir. She folds subjective experiences of dread into projected scenarios of immiseration, collective disempowerment, and likely violence—an unavoidable conclusion except by treading a narrow path whose coordinates she concedes are hard to discern. David Wallace-Welles's *The Uninhabited Earth* (2019) and Geoff Mann and Joel Wainwright's *Climate Leviathan* (2018) follows this model, as does David Runciman's *How Democracy Ends* (2018).

In Zuboff's case, the story begins with her family's house burning down and her efforts to reconstruct a sense of home in its wake. The death of her husband, to whom the book is dedicated, as well as her German editor, Frank Schirrmacher, also cast an understandably long shadow. Her 688-page book is often less analysis than gut-wrenching scream—a sometimes moving, often exasperating, attempt at mourning what she sees as a passing relationship to our innermost selves.

She implores us to fight the "coup from above" being staged by Google and other tech giants. The book is self-conscious agitprop, designed to "rekindle the sense of outrage and loss over what is being taken from us." It resonates with the ash-sifting moment around the end of World War II, and there are analogies to the highly personal political interventions of Friedrich Hayek's *The Road to Serfdom* (1944), B. F. Skinner's *Walden Two* (1948), and Hannah Arendt's *Origins of Totalitarianism* (1951). Indeed, Zuboff likens herself to Arendt, plumbing the present to find the origins of a new threat which, like totalitarianism, is all-consuming but which takes the new forms of a "muted, sanitized tyranny."

Zuboff brings different weapons to the effort, however. Occasionally, she reprises her life as a business school professor to offer facts about corporate governance. When Google went public in 2004, for example, it introduced a dual-class stock structure that preserved extra voting rights for founders. Imitated by Facebook, Tesla, Snap, and, more recently, Lyft and Pinterest, this model—which concentrates power and decreases shareholder voice—has become an industry standard.

Although Zuboff uses the example of Cambridge Analytica, her alarm bells were ringing before Donald Trump and Brexit. She plumbs earlier history, pointing out that Barack Obama was the "Google President," appearing next to Eric Schmidt at his first postelection press conference in 2008. Even further back, the CIA's attempt to "swim in [Silicon] Valley," as George Tenet declared in 1997, led to the weaponization of the surveillance capacities of tech and communications firms and investment in start-ups with ominous names such as Recorded Future. First drafts of Zuboff's arguments appeared in the *Frankfurter Allgemeine Zeitung* after Edward Snowden's jaw-dropping revelations about the scope of incursions into privacy under a Democratic administration. Since then, she has helped fuel a debate about tech and privacy in Germany that continues to be more wide-ranging and deeply-felt than in North America.

Yet Zuboff's preferred weapon in the end is neither the factoid nor the FOIA revelation but the metaphor. Over hundreds of pages, the book proceeds as a kind of internal arms race in the quest for ever more extreme ways to convey what is happening. We begin by finding that we "are the objects from which raw materials are extracted and expropriated," trapped in a "dispossession cycle." Then we are an "extraction quarry." For a while, "we are the native peoples . . . whose tacit claims to self-determination have vanished from the maps of our own experience," and the terms of service we click through are the rebooted *requerimiento* of the conquistadors, read to us in an incomprehensible language before our enserfment.

Our utter lack of agency is emphasized time and again: "unruly life is brought to heel, rendered as behavioral data and reimagined as a territory for browsing, searching, knowing, and modifying" as "the prediction imperative unleashes the surveillance hounds to stalk behavior from the depths." It may even already be too late: "The world is vanquished now, on its knees, and brought to you by Google." In the metaphorical coup de grâce, she pronounces our own extinction: "You are not the product; you are the abandoned carcass."

Where to begin? Applying the normal tools of interpretation to such William Burroughs–like spiraling almost seems inappropriate. One could point out her excessive stagism, which implies we have moved from one form of capitalism to another without acknowledging their coexistence. What of, for example, the real indigenous people who are still subjected to real extraction? Is this not happening alongside the metaphorical kind involved in ad targeting, itself a pretty minor part of the economy writ large even if a site of tremendous growth?

One could ask whether her description does not flunk the Cultural Studies 101 test by failing to acknowledge that the media's designers do not dictate directly its use and consumption. We hear a great deal about what companies "aim" to do through baroque projects of "behavioral modification," but, as with the Cold War brainwashing techniques she references, we have little evidence that these efforts work—except for generating ever greater contracts for those pronouncing their own effectiveness. Pokémon Go was a startlingly popular trend, but was it really "a public announcement of history-illuminating change that moves through us and among us, irreversibly altering life as we have known it"?

One could point out that surveillance might not be an apt metaphor as we are not rendered supine, as so many of her metaphors imply, but encouraged always to emote, rage, flame, heart, rant, stan, and swoon. Is it not more like incitement capitalism? Isn't the precise characteristic—the secret even—of this mode of accumulation that we are not actually dispossessed or extracted, but that we get to keep our own feelings even as Google gets them too?

Zuboff offers examples that undermine her own point in passing. A family falls on hard times and misses car payments. Someone starts an online fundraising appeal to "pay off the Kippings' car, detail it, purchase a Thanksgiving turkey, and give the couple an additional gift of $1,000." We are presented this Upworthy anecdote as evidence of what is being lost in the present "dystopian rule of the uncontract." Indeed, Zuboff has painted herself into such a corner that she can only bear witness to the scattered husks of our formerly rich lives; she cannot concede that this salutary form of sociability emerged online, using the precise tools and platforms of surveillance capitalism she condemns.

In another subtly undermining case, Zuboff recounts a study where subjects are shown how much of their location data is sent to tech companies. After the study, 58 percent restricted permissions on their apps. But she fails to dwell on the inverse: after getting the kind of direct information that few users ever will, 42 percent did not. The lesson seems to be—if we needed any reminding in the long post-Snowden shrug—that old-fashioned enlightenment is not enough to enrage.

Perhaps the most recurrent metaphor Zuboff uses in her quest to astonish is that of darkness. The "dark data continent of your inner life" is "summoned into the light for others' profit." "All that is moist and alive must hand over its facts," she writes, "there can be no shadow, no darkness." Here, too, we can see the outlines of her prescription of a solution. As in the metaphor of surveillance, the problem is the one-way relationship. Tech companies operate in the shadows of public oversight even as they subject our inner lives to the klieg lights of the prison yard, approaching what she calls "a collectivist vision that claims the totality of society."

It follows that the solution is to drain the darkness, spin around the interrogation lamp, and expose the tech companies themselves to the light of publicity. Here, the law plays the key role. She hopes that social movements can make "the life of the law . . . move against surveillance capitalism." What will this look like? Her repeated metaphor of the Berlin Wall seems inapt. There is no territorial West Germany into which we can all burst. Yet she feels Europe still offers some hope. She cites the EU's General Data Protection Regulation (GDPR) as a sign that a white horse may arrive yet to stay Google's death hand. After we virtual natives have had the virtual land of our souls seized, we must summon the will to hail the sheriff and the judge.

WALTER MATTLI SHARES a similar faith in the law as antidote to darkness in his book on the changing nature of stock market governance. In a crisp 178 pages (which even finds space for some repetition), *Darkness by Design: The Hidden Power of Global Capital Markets* (2019) tells the story of what was once the undisputed throne room of global finance: the New York Stock Exchange.

Created in 1869 with 1,060 members, the NYSE only added 40 seats before 1929 when, to the sound of a sad trombone, it increased its membership by 25 percent a few months before the stock market crashed. Mattli is bullish about this early exchange and even more about the one that followed after 1945.

In his description, the stock exchange had something of the horizontality of other archetypical sites of U.S. democracy: the village green or the New England town hall. "It was a body of many voices and no single one was dominant or prevailed," Mattli writes. He does not hesitate to use the D-word itself: the NYSE was a "democratic private governance system where all members had an equal voice on key matters."

Just as Zuboff sees the mid-century management of Henry Ford and Arthur Sloane as models of class compromise and the redistribution of the rewards of economic growth, Mattli sees the

NYSE up until the 1990s as good capitalism: a place where finance could serve valuable social functions by processing information and directing capital to where it was most efficiently put to use.

Yet in an ironic counterpoint to Zuboff's book, the hero of Mattli's story is literally surveillance. Much of the book is taken up with describing how the creation of a Market Surveillance unit in the 1930s provided continuous oversight on the trading floor, which, until the advent of digital trading, remained a literal place.

"Floor cops" appointed by the exchange's governing body circulated and ensured an "orderly market." The space of the trading floor also allowed for mutual surveillance, a kind of Jane Jacobs model of financial governance whereby traders watched their neighbors and remained aware of the importance of reputation and the value of their brand.

Reports were filed and infractions were punished, but Mattli emphasizes the self-governing quality of the exchange above all else in the golden age. Questions of economic distribution and equality beyond the peculiar demos of the exchange (and the kind of worlds that finance created) are beyond Mattli's analysis, but he makes much of the fact that the membership was relatively equal in its capitalization internally, with no member of the stock exchange being radically richer than the others.

Everything changed with the introduction of the computer in the 1970s. At first, the computer seemed to enhance the powers of surveillance, reducing the time spent on "reconstructing a day's trading activity" from weeks to "days or even hours" and introducing an "electronic Audit Trail" by the 1980s. Some traders recoiled at this. "It seems like we live in the world of Big Brother," one complained.

But soon, the wheel turned. "By the late 1990s, over 90 percent of NYSE trades were handled electronically," Mattli writes. With the advent of high-frequency trading by the 2000s, it became possible to outrun the regulators. Traders could use the bazooka-like power of their computers to manipulate prices by "quote stuffing," which could mean "placing and canceling . . . over 25,000 orders of a stock per second" or "spoofing," sending orders to simulate momentum on a particular stock. The sheer data demands of reconstructing the course of investment became overwhelming, as did the time frames involved in spotting an infraction. Clocks would have to be "synchronized to nanosecond accuracy to enable regulators to reconstruct market events."

More consequential was the choice of the NYSE to renege on its once hallowed duty of market surveillance altogether, slashing its market surveillance division by two thirds in 2007 before outsourcing it all to a third party a few years later. The impetus was not so much an ideological conversion to market fundamentalism but the pragmatic fear of losing their biggest members as new exchanges allowed the threat of exit to create an evermore trader-friendly and regulator-unfriendly atmosphere.

Mattli shows how the shape of financial governance—and lack thereof—was pushed by a small elite of investment entities. The advantages gained by those able to make costly investments in computerization began to concentrate wealth at the upper end of the exchange's members, including the "national commercial and non-U.S. 'universal' banks" that deregulation had allowed to enter. By 2000 the twenty-five second-tier firms had less than

10 percent of the market capitalization of the top ten. Household-name titans such as Barclays, Credit Suisse, Citigroup, Deutsche Bank, Goldman Sachs, Merrill Lynch, Morgan Stanley, and JP Morgan dominated.

In the new millennium, Mattli's beloved "market democracy" was degenerating into oligarchy. Enabling this was not only the unequal access to expensive technology but also the new tendency of big firms to transact beyond the public eye of the financial agora. Here the metaphor of darkness returns.

"Dark pools" is a term used to describe a venue where trades are made without displaying "price order or order size information." The volume of dark trading "tripled in less than a decade to about 37 percent of all trading in 2017." Mattli hastens to point out their potential usefulness, since dark pools are intended primarily for institutional investors whose bids might otherwise overly disrupt the market. The spread of dark pools points to two facts: first, the increasing size of investment firms large enough to handle enormous transactions internally; and two, our collective participation in the very world that Mattli is describing.

What transpired on the trading floors and in the microwave-borne flashes of the exchange may be only relevant to clients, but by the early twenty-first century, we were almost all clients. Recalling Julia Ott's research on how *Wall Street Met Main Street* (2014), Mattli points out how, already by 1930, a third of U.S. households were shareholders. By the 1990s, 401(k)s and pension funds were a huge part of the investment picture. Over half of Americans currently own stock either individually or as part of a fund.

In other words, those operating on Wall Street may often be part of the 1 percent, but the wealth they are handling belongs to all of us. This makes Mattli's descriptions and prescriptions of acute interest, partially because what he is describing can seriously exacerbate risk and, as we have been shown repeatedly, risk is privatized in good times and socialized in times of crisis (such as after 2008).

The question, though, is whether Mattli's appeal to Louis Brandeis's refrain that "sunlight is the best disinfectant" is enough. Here the question is the same as the one we could ask of Zuboff: How golden shone the Golden Age of Capitalism? Is it utopian enough to imagine a return to that period of robust Fordism when the United States was the engine of the world economy, exporting industrial products globally to former enemies tucked snugly under its nuclear umbrella?

Zuboff's description of the capacity of tech companies for "total information . . . and the promise of guaranteed outcomes" is notable in how close it comes to discussions dating back to the Socialist Calculation Debates in interwar Vienna about technologically enabled models of socialist planning. Would it be possible to turn the wheel once again to see how the power of computerization can be socialized and turned toward the problems we face—problems that are fundamentally different than those of the 1950s? Such new horizons would offer a vision to chain Zuboff's rekindled astonishment to something other than the mid-century Golden Age or what proved in many ways to be the false dawn after the Berlin Wall's fall.

MAPPING SUCH A FUTURE requires being clear-eyed about the tools at hand. A third book is invaluable for its (near) break with the constraints imposed by the binary of darkness and light—and while orders of magnitude more understated than Zuboff's, Katharina Pistor's *The Code of Capital: How the Law Creates Wealth and Inequality* (2019) is also an urgent tract. The difference, in her telling, is that the law doesn't always ride a white horse. It comes as often to perpetuate injustice as redress it.

One of the misleading visions of the last thirty years of globalization is the clip-art image of a gridded globe, streaked by laser beams of information and money. Beyond the proliferation of obstacles to mobility repressed by this image, it also gives the false sense of capital existing mostly in low Earth orbit beyond the reach of territorial nation-states—an extraterrestrial "market people" beaming from one spot to the next. Some critics of the present order reinforce this image by speaking of a world where the market has become "disembedded" from society and states, cut free of institutional constraints to chase profits and transmit them back into the bank accounts of the "few not the many."

But while the outcome might be accurate, Pistor makes clear that the description is faulty. Assets—and wealth itself—do not exist outside the law and the state. The concentration of wealth, and its evasion of state attempts at capture through taxation, also do not happen by escaping law or the state, but *through* the law and the state—through projects of legal "encoding," to use Pistor's dominant metaphor.

The protagonists of Pistor's narrative include the trust, which is used to put assets an arm's length from their original owner (originally to family members, but now, increasingly, to financial intermediaries); the partitioning of asset pools within corporations, which allows them (as in Mattli) to take on extra risk and avoid shareholder governance; and the Investor State Dispute Settlement mechanism, which allows foreign investors to sue states for lost profits.

She shows that capital is global not because it exists in the ether, but because, when properly legally framed, it is portable: "it is possible to code assets in the modules of one legal system and still have them respected and enforced by courts and regulators of another country." Far from a sub-galactic global space of flows, she shows that assets are almost all drawn up according to the templates of two relatively small places, New York and Great Britain.

Corporations may be able to choose their own "birthplace," but that birthplace must still be on the planet. The place where the asset comes to Earth points to the place where it can (at least hypothetically) be challenged. Pistor introduces us to new sites and conventions created to offer protection for capital mobility and insulation from democratic states, places with their own acronyms, where P.R.I.M.E. Finance (Panel of Recognized International Market Experts in Finance) protects PRIMA (the Place of Relevant Intermediary Approach convention).

The quicksilver quality of assets can be a strength but also a weakness. While Zuboff presents human behavior as the novel "fourth fictional commodity" now being enclosed after Karl Polanyi's land, labor, and money, Pistor points out that immaterial or intangible property have long presented a challenge to capitalists eager to turn a song, a swoosh, a swipe, or a string of formula into private property. Pistor reminds us that Google not only seeks to elude the law, but also use it. Its algorithm, PageRank—which is "best described as a filing system"—was patented and exclusively licensed, and it practices aggressive uses of trade secrecy law and noncompete clauses.

While Zuboff uses metaphors of darkness to describe tech capitalism, Pistor uses a metaphor from tech to describe capitalism's laws. A terrain of struggle populated by "modules" and "coding" holds neither the liberatory promise of eruption into the benevolently regulated space beyond the East Germany of our own digital abjection, nor the royal road back to the financial agora of the mid-century stock exchange. Instead it is a workaday exploration of strategies necessary to redefine what property is in the first place.

This struggle does not happen on level ground. The capacity to engage in legal combat is entirely conditioned by access to resources—the teams of lawyers that can be deployed. The volume of these resources themselves is an expression of the accumulation of the concentrations of wealth created in the last couple of centuries, making path dependency a powerful force to be reckoned with.

Here, Pistor's example of Belize is instructive. In 2007 Mayan people, with the help of a team of historians, lawyers, and anthropologists, won a supreme court case establishing the collective property right of indigenous people to their own land. But their victory was short-lived. The government soon trampled on its own court's ruling by allowing mining by private corporations. The example is either hopeful or fatalistic, depending on your disposition, but it remains a valuable case study in how property claims are made and unmade. As Pistor points out, there are few claims more powerful at present than that something is "legal" and that it is "property." Yet, as her book shows, neither of these claims are universal and both dissolve on exposure to history. Her metaphors allow us to see how, by ceding democratic control of law, we have "depoliticized critical questions of self-governance," preserving mobility for some and blocking it for others.

It also reminds us that ideas of wild, ungoverned spaces of data and finance as depicted by Zuboff and Mattli are false. The wealth drawn from both the digital darkness and the dark pools of Wall Street exists only by virtue of the law's encasement. Draining the darkness would only bring to light something we already knew was there. What we face is less a long night awaiting the arrival of light and more a war of movement along long-established trench lines. Suns rise by themselves; recoding takes work.

FREE SPEECH, INCORPORATED
Amy Kapczynski

THE FIRST AMENDMENT has long been celebrated as the guardian of our democracy, a protector of the robust public discourse essential to self-determination. Today, however, the First Amendment is being shaped into something very different: a guardian of the interests of private companies that resist democratic regulation.

Many are familiar with Supreme Court cases such as *Citizens United v. Federal Election Commission* (2010) that use the First Amendment as a weapon against campaign finance restrictions. Others may also have heard of the 2018 decision *Janus v. AFSCME*, which struck a grave blow to public sector unions. In that case, a 5–4 majority flatly reversed more than 40 years of precedent, barring certain dues (so-called "fair-share fees") on the grounds that they conflict with union members' speech rights. What has largely escaped public notice, though, is that the Supreme Court has also begun reshaping the First Amendment into a tool to broadly undermine the regulatory state. Today, most Americans are clamoring for more robust regulation of markets. But what companies cannot win through democratic politics, they are hoping to win from increasingly conservative courts, with First Amendment speech protections as an increasingly powerful weapon in their arsenal.

In a 2017 case, for example, five merchants challenged a New York law preventing businesses from adding a surcharge on credit card purchases. They did not argue that it was bad for business, or bad for consumers, or bad public policy, or a restriction on contractual liberty. Instead, they argued it violated their *speech rights* by regulating how they communicated with customers about prices. The Supreme Court agreed, sending it back to the lower court for review. Consider, as well, laws requiring companies to disclose whether they are trading in conflict diamonds, or mandating graphic warning labels on cigarettes. They, too, have been overturned for violating companies' speech rights. As Justice Stephen Breyer wrote in a case last term, "Because much, perhaps most, human behavior takes place through speech," the Supreme Court's new approach to free speech law threatens a wave of new lawsuits "over the constitutional validity of much, perhaps most, government regulation."

Particularly troubling are new First Amendment cases that chip away at the power of the U.S. Food and Drug Administration (FDA). Do drug companies have to provide scientifically reliable evidence for their claims to the agency before marketing a medicine? Do e-cigarette companies have to show that their products have health benefits before marketing them that way? For as long as we have had a regulatory state, these kinds of questions have been the domain of Congress and regulators. Today, courts are increasingly treating them as constitutional questions, answering them through a First Amendment doctrine that treats many forms of regulation as the illegitimate coercion of speech, rather than as the democratic prerogative of a public seeking to protect itself from the risks of deception and harm inherent to market society.

We have been here before, during the dark history of the Supreme Court's Lochner Era (1890–1937). For more than four decades—extending well into the Depression—the Supreme Court effectively wrote laissez-faire economics into the Constitution by repeatedly striking down laws regulating working hours and conditions or seeking to stabilize the national economy. According to the Court, these laws and ordinances were illegitimate intrusions on the rights of contract. In 1937 the Court—wildly out of step with public sentiment and in the face of Franklin Roosevelt's court-packing threat—retreated, and a new settlement was forged: courts would use their authority to reinforce democracy, focusing on voting rights, speech protections, discrimination, and other protections for vulnerable groups, leaving ordinary socioeconomic legislation to elected officials. The current Court, armed with a new interpretation of the First Amendment, is eroding that settlement. In the process, it is undermining our collective authority to solve critically important social problems and casting into doubt the fundamental structure of our regulatory state.

CONSIDER THE CASE of Alfred Caronia, a sales representative for Jazz Pharmaceuticals, which manufactures the drug Xyrem. The main ingredient of Xyrem is a form of GHB, a central nervous system depressant notorious for its use as a date-rape drug. The drug has FDA approval only for the treatment of two kinds of narcolepsy in adults, and drugs with small patient populations—especially drugs as dangerous as Xyrem—generally do not sell well. So Jazz Pharmaceuticals did what many other companies in its shoes have done: it launched a marketing offensive. Alfred Caronia was one of the ground soldiers in this effort—and the one unlucky enough to be caught on tape in a federal sting. According to the trial transcript, he urged doctors to prescribe Xyrem for a long litany of ills: fibromyalgia, chronic pain, fatigue, restless leg syndrome. There is "no safer drug," he declared, even recommending it for children as young as four. Caronia was convicted in 2008 under the Food and Drug Cosmetic Act (FDCA), New Deal legislation from 1938 which gave the FDA its powers. His efforts as a sales representative to market off-label uses of Xyrem were found to violate the FDCA's prohibitions on "misbranding" drugs.

What Caronia did was illegal because, since the 1960s, the FDA has required that companies prove, *before* marketing a drug, that it is safe and effective for a specific use. (Doctors can prescribe drugs for off-label uses, but manufacturers were not supposed to market them for those uses.) This is because a drug's side effects and efficacy can change in different patient populations—for example, in the young or the old—and for different kinds of uses. Addiction or overdose may be tolerable risks for a painkiller intended for terminal cancer patients, but not for those in mild pain.

Our modern drug regulation and innovation system relies on these marketing restrictions. Because they cannot promote medicines without showing that they work, companies conduct and hand over the clinical research the FDA and medical experts use to evaluate a drug's effects. This powerful system of premarket review grew in response to a series of disasters, each revealing new risks in laissez-faire approaches to markets in food and medicine. By the early 1900s, markets in food and medicine had become increasingly anonymous and far-reaching, and profit-motivated sellers had found ways to hawk their wares that gravely endangered the public. While the patent medicine industry seized upon newspaper advertising, promising miracle cures but usually delivering nothing more than alcohol, opioids, or worse, food marketers discovered that suffusing food with borax and formaldehyde lengthened shelf life. Upton Sinclair's *The Jungle* (1906) still provides the most indelible image of modern capitalism without a regulatory state: workmen slipping into a vat and emerging from the factory pressed into a packet of "Durham's Pure Leaf Lard."

Recognizing that only a federal regulatory agency could assert control over the risks of these newly nationalizing markets, Congress created the FDA in 1906. Sellers would now be required to accurately label their wares and disclose ingredients such as opioids. After a patent medicine called Elixir Sulfanilamide killed dozens around the country, Congress in 1938 gave the agency authority beyond labeling and disclosure requirements, allowing it to bar dangerous products from the market. Then came Thalidomide. Prescribed widely in Europe for morning sickness in pregnancy, the drug turned out to cause horrible birth defects. *LIFE* published images of children with shortened or missing limbs, and the press celebrated the story of a regulator at the FDA who, through extraordinary persistence, prevented the drug's approval in the United States. The outcry turned into a mandate for one of the most muscular regulatory agencies in the country and the world. By the 1960s, it was settled: pharmaceutical companies would have to provide robust, scientifically reliable evidence *before* marketing their wares.

Hence Caronia's legal troubles: he was promoting Xyrem for uses for which it had never been approved and so violated the FDCA's prohibitions on "misbranding" drugs. In the end, though, he was saved by the Supreme Court's ruling in a new First Amendment case, *Sorrell v. IMS Health* (2011), to which I'll return at length. After that decision, Caronia appealed his case, arguing that he was simply exercising his right to *free speech* when he marketed Xyrem for off-label uses. The U.S. Court of Appeals for the Second Circuit concluded that the Supreme Court's new precedent was in conflict with six decades of FDA regulatory authority. Caronia won his appeal, and the First Amendment was at war with democratic regulation.

What caused this shift in the Court's opinion, and where are we headed next?

THE FIRST AMENDMENT declares that Congress "shall make no law . . . abridging the freedom of speech, or of the press." Taken literally, these words would render government as we know it impossible. But courts have never taken them literally. People are penalized every day—they are put in jail, they lose their livelihoods—because of the words they utter. Doctors are liable for what they say to their patients, and if you lie to investigators you can be charged with perjury. The government bars witnesses in lawsuits from giving expert testimony about phrenology and astrology. Companies are required to disclose certain risks to investors and are subject to the law of fraud, a crime often consummated entirely through speech. To bar a sale of something is to restrict speech, because offers for sale are speech. And what does the law of contracts regulate if not words?

Buried here is a basic point about legal interpretation. Does a ban on "vehicles in the park" prevent a parks commission from permitting baby strollers or a decommissioned tank? You cannot decide unless you have a sense of the purpose of the ban. This general point applies to the First Amendment, too. Courts need a sense of the purpose of the constitutional free speech guarantee in order to determine how far they should reach into the power to legislate. Courts only began to assert free speech protections in a serious way in the 1920s, and since then have often emphasized the importance of speech protections for democratic governance.

We protect speech in order to facilitate "public discourse." First Amendment law is centrally about protecting the formation of public opinion because, as Robert Post has described, only if we can freely speak in public can we understand and render our government legitimately our own. As Justice Louis Brandeis once put it, "The right of a citizen of the United States to take part, for his own or the country's benefit, in the making of federal laws and in the conduct of the government, necessarily includes the right to speak or write about them; to endeavor to make his own opinion concerning laws existing or contemplated prevail; and, to this end, to teach the truth as he sees it."

One consequence of the Court's democratic focus was that, for decades, it simply did not apply the First Amendment to commercial speech—just as today it still does not apply it to the rules of evidence or to the law of contracts. As Justice Hugo Black, one of the Court's early champions of the modern conception of free speech, succinctly put it, the First Amendment had nothing to do with a "merchant who goes from door to door selling pots."

This all changed in the 1970s, when the Supreme Court decided that commercial speech in fact did warrant constitutional protection. In striking down a state law barring pharmacists from advertising the prices of prescription drugs, the Court announced that "the free flow of commercial information is indispensable . . . to the proper allocation of resources in a free enterprise system" and "also indispensable to the formation of intelligent opinions as to how that system ought to be regulated or altered." The First Amendment protects commercial speech, the Court declared, not out of a concern for the speakers, but because *listeners* need that information for public decision-making. A new spirit was on the move through our law.

This listener-based argument felt a little strained, and no one was more unsparing about its shortcomings than Justice William Rehnquist, a Richard Nixon appointee and leading conservative: Americans may "regard the choice of shampoo as just as important as who may be elected to local, state, or national political office," he scoffed, "but that does not automatically bring information about competing shampoos within the protection of the First Amendment." What kind of world was the Court ushering in, he asked? One where a pharmacist might run an ad in the local paper saying, as he put it, "Don't spend another sleepless night. Ask your doctor to prescribe Seconal without delay"?

You likely know how this story ends. That decision, *Virginia State Pharmacy Board v. Virginia Citizens Consumer Council* (1976), did indeed help to unleash direct-to-consumer advertising of drugs, by ensuring that something that is illegal in most of the world could not be barred here. It also gave ammunition to industry-funded conservative legal groups such as the Washington Legal Foundation. Though the cases received little attention at the time, the group used the new commercial speech doctrine to slowly deregulate drug and dietary supplement advertising.

It was not until the 1990s, however, that conservative justices realized the true power of the First Amendment to undermine the regulatory state. By 1995 Rehnquist, who had been so appalled at the notion of crass drug advertising in the 1970s, joined the Court in invalidating restrictions on putting alcohol content on beer labels. In a wave of subsequent decisions, a new polarity emerged, with the Court's conservative wing deploying the First Amendment in more and more cases to strike down ordinary economic regulation.

In 2011 the commercial speech train jumped the tracks. The legal argument shifted decisively from its earlier focus on citizens' need for information and toward a newfound solicitude for the rights of corporate speakers. In *Sorrell v. IMS Health*, the Supreme Court sided with pharmaceutical companies against a Vermont law passed to protect doctors from intrusive pharmaceutical marketers. The Vermont law required doctors to affirmatively consent before the details of their prescribing practices could be sold to data miners and then used by the Alfred Caronias of the world to badger them into prescribing more and more. The law had some sensible exceptions though—academic researchers could access the data more easily, for example.

The exceptions killed the rule. Fixating on the fact that some parties could more easily access and use data about doctors' prescribing practices than others, the Supreme Court found that the Vermont law was not a sensible protection of doctors and patients but was unconstitutionally *discriminating* against companies. The law not only overtly disfavored marketing as a kind of speech and so regulated by reference to "content"—long a warning flag where political speech regulations were concerned—but also "disfavors specific speakers, namely pharmaceutical manufacturers."

What could this possibly have to do with upholding democracy? This was one of the critical questions posed by *Sorrell v. IMS Health*, and the majority opinion, written by Justice Anthony Kennedy, simply sailed past it. The majority also routed around the broad framework of analysis that the Court had used for decades to distinguish restrictions on commercial speech from restrictions on political speech. Under that framework, lawmakers can, for example, bar false and misleading commercial speech outright. In contrast, lies are protected in politics, and Congress will rarely be able to impose restrictions turning on a political viewpoint: for example, applying restrictions to pro-life arguments that are not applied to pro-choice ones. Even true and non-misleading commercial speech can be regulated, if the government had a substantial interest and the law directly advanced that interest.

In *Sorrell*, the Court cast doubt on this historical approach, introducing into the mix a new set of questions about content neutrality and viewpoint discrimination. In dissent, Justice Stephen Breyer sounded the alarm: the Court was opening an avenue to meddle in an extraordinary range of legislative and regulatory decisions. Regulators often train their attention on some subjects and not others. Cosmetic companies, for example, might be required to substantiate the claim that a "product contains 'cleansing grains that scrub away dirt and excess oil'" while "opponents of cosmetics use need not substantiate their claims." Appliance companies might be required to publicize ways to save energy, though their industrial counterparts are not. Or, the FDA might forbid drug companies from promoting drugs for unapproved uses, though academic researchers may recommend for or against the same uses.

Untethered from its historical moorings, Breyer argued, this new First Amendment threatened to undermine the historical deference given to legislatures to govern "ordinary commercial or regulatory legislation." He was referring to the great Lochner settlement, the one that brought the Court back from the brink of disaster in the 1930s. From the ashes, constitutional lawyers had to construct a new sense of what courts were for and a new argument for why courts should be allowed to overturn the judgments of elected bodies. They landed on the idea that an essential part of their purpose was to protect democratic self-government, by protecting speech, ensuring voting rights, and making sure that all voices—including minorities who might be excluded—were heard in the process. The way they distinguished the new order from the constitutional cliff that Lochner had driven the Court toward was in what they *wouldn't* do: the Court no longer had a role in second-guessing the judgment of Congress when it passes ordinary socioeconomic laws. That was outside of the competency of courts and a domain left to the people.

The new First Amendment is undoing this settlement. And implicit in the language of discrimination that has consolidated among the conservative justices lies an account as to why: the problem is that the people are disrupting efficient markets and discriminating against corporations. To protect against this, the First Amendment today has become a new kind of "guardian of our democracy"—a guardian of we the pharmaceutical companies, we the gun salesmen, we the e-cigarette makers.

THE CASES NOW BEING LITIGATED by conservative legal groups and industry paint a grim picture of where we might be headed. For years, conservative legal groups have railed against occupational licensing. These are the rules that require training and exams for teachers, lawyers, and doctors and that, in extreme cases, permit professionals to be sanctioned, including by losing their ability to practice. All of these restrict efficiency from the perspective of a neoclassical economics that assumes markets are replete with good information and that disavows any role for groups in the cultivation of something like virtue or professional expertise.

If you want to wage a successful litigation campaign, the rule is to start small, with sympathetic plaintiffs. In the licensing contest, the camel's nose is made of tour guides and tire engineers. To impose licensing requirements on these professionals, conservative advocacy groups argue, is to prohibit speech about monuments and tire treads (content regulation). And it is discriminatory, because tour guides and tire engineers are forbidden to say things that other people are allowed to discuss freely. Federal appeals courts in the last few years have come to agree.

Last term, Justice Clarence Thomas put the pedal to the floor with one sentence in a case about crisis pregnancy centers. Speaking for a majority of five, he declared, "This Court's precedents do not recognize such a tradition for a category called 'professional speech'." In a pen stroke, he wiped out decisions in lower courts that had for years treated professional speech regulations as exempt from First Amendment review.

Next stop: if the state cannot prevent tour guides from speaking without a license, why can it stop teachers and veterinarians? And then, why can states prevent someone from giving medical or legal advice without a license? These are precisely the questions coming to the fore, through cleverly designed cases, each intended to take us another step down this road, eventually leading to the explicit deregulation of the professions. Even the Lochner court did not tread this far. Over and over, at a time when laissez-faire reigned, it yielded to states' authority to regulate professions such as medicine. "There is no right to practice medicine," the Court declared, "which is not subordinate to the police power of the States."

Corporate disclosures are a target, too. Can we compel companies to inform us, for example, what is in their products and the conditions under which they are made? Such reporting was long considered unproblematic, because protections of commercial speech were supposed to be about protecting *listeners*, not speakers. You and I cannot be forced, in contrast, to salute the flag or to avow even true statements about our political beliefs. That, the Court has long concluded, would implicate our autonomy as citizens. But even this distinction is eroding as courts are coming to treat corporations as speakers whose integrity can be undermined if they are forced to speak in a voice that is not theirs. "Uncontroversial" factual disclosures are allowed, but nothing that smacks of "opinions."

You don't need a high-priced corporate lawyer to drive a wide-bodied truck through this opening. A few years back, the D.C. Circuit Court of Appeals struck down a requirement that companies report whether their gems were obtained from conflict zones in the Democratic Republic of Congo (DRC). And tobacco companies won a major victory striking down the FDA's graphic warning labels on cigarettes. Both measures, courts concluded, illegitimately compelled commercial speech. If democratically elected officials cannot require a Jehovah's Witness to salute the flag, how can they require a large mining company to speak to something as "controversial" as whether its operations might be supporting violence in the DRC? That is the new First Amendment at work.

In fact, every labeling and advertising law for every commodity is now in the crosshairs. Calorie disclosures: do they overemphasize calories, undermining a company's right to convey a happier image about its products? Does a required warning about cell phone radiation disrupt corporate messaging and so run afoul of the Constitution? What about sugar warnings? Companies have pushed all of these arguments in the courts—so far with limited success. But attuned to the power of the small businessman in the American imagination and looking ahead to the growing wave of Federalist Society judges appointed by Trump, right-wing litigation shops are building an army of more sympathetic complainants. They chose, for example, the South Mountain Creamery for their assault on the FDA's authority over product labels. The farmers asked a seemingly innocuous question: How can the FDA mandate that the business call its skim milk "imitation," when it has, in fact, skimmed the fat off the top of whole milk? The FDA has long required that food products be labeled "imitation" when essential nutrients are removed in processes such as skimming but are not restored. What is masquerading as a narrow challenge to labeling requirements for the benefit of small dairy farmers is in reality a wholesale offensive against the FDA's ability to protect shoppers from foods misleadingly lacking the nutritional value people have come to associate with them. (The case is still pending.)

Ordinary economic transactions also involve speech, so they too are at risk. This seems fantastic but consider the case of *Nordyke v. Santa Clara County* (1996). In it, a federal district court ruled that Santa Clara's attempt to forbid gun sales at its fairgrounds was an infringement on speech. As the district court said, "a gun may not be sold in silence, without any exchange of verbal communication whatsoever." Once this was defined as an issue of *speech*, the court was empowered to ask about its justification: Why ban sales at the fair and not at the gun shop down the street? Finding the lawmaker's proof lacking, the court threw the law out. When appealed, the case was upheld on a similar logic: the county was regulating speech and had not provided sufficient evidence for its choice.

Some of the laws being targeted may be unnecessary, even idiotic. But whether credit card surcharges or skim milk labeling rules are stupid has never in the modern era been a *constitutional* question. Rather, the question was, who decides? And the answer was, emphatically, the people through the officials they elect. Recall that constitutional obligations cannot be revised except by constitutional amendment—or by a reshaped Supreme Court.

The stakes for our democracy are deep. But so too are the stakes for our safety. Among the most pernicious cases are those targeting the FDA's powers over the tobacco and pharmaceutical industry, threatening return to a world in which we know little about the drugs we put in our bodies and snake-oil salesmen reign supreme. In its ruling in favor of Caronia, the Second Circuit made much of the fact that doctors are allowed to prescribe off label, though companies may not promote off label—here again was the dreaded "discrimination." In context, though, the differentiation makes sense. The regulatory scheme is about the production of evidence, and it is drug companies, and not individual doctors, that are in a position to fund and conduct the studies needed to guide practice. Our pharmaceutical industry was built—thrived, in fact—under a strong regulatory thumb: companies had to provide high-quality evidence or stay out of the market. But if it costs less to run catchy ad campaigns than to run studies, drug companies will choose that path every time.

The *Caronia* case still permits the FDA to bar false and misleading marketing. But it ensures the people who judge that fact will have neither the evidence nor the expertise to make good on that task. In a follow-up case to *Caronia*, a federal district court judge overruled the FDA, permitting a company to market a fish oil pill to a broad, low-risk population as a heart disease remedy. The FDA argued that the pill did nothing for that group. But without the benefit of fact-finding or expert witnesses, the judge disagreed. This was the same judge who, during the hearing, said to the lawyers: "You're talking to somebody who has difficulty using a toaster. I'm the last person who should opine on this."

Lining up after the pharmaceutical industry are the e-cigarette makers. They are targeting a federal law that requires them to provide evidence before they claim their products are lower risk than conventional cigarettes. The law was passed after Congress found that tobacco companies had misled the public for years, marketing "low tar" and "light" cigarettes that offer no health benefits. But a wave of current lawsuits argues that the Constitution forbids Congress and the FDA from learning from this dark history and from demanding evidence before a new generation is addicted.

Consider, finally, the implications of the new First Amendment for a world where so much is digital, mediated by software and measured in terabytes. What is a file that instructs a 3D printer how to make a gun? Speech, of course. That is the argument made by Defense Distributed, a nonprofit that makes executable CAD files for plastic pistols and

AR-15 components that can be printed from the comfort of your home. The State Department, citing a law designed to prevent the export of certain weapons, asked the company to remove the files from the Internet. The company sued, pointing to its First Amendment rights to speech. A lower court deferred the question, and shortly thereafter, the Trump administration settled the suit, voluntarily agreeing to let the files be disseminated around the world.

Are we a people with the authority to hold market actors accountable? Or are we in a new era, our sovereignty transferred to their sovereignty? Will "Congress shall make no law" come to mean no effective law against commercial fraud and no effective regulation against the addictive and toxic products that companies slide into the stream of commerce? The minorities that courts once understood as underrepresented persons are now marginalized corporations, and the power that they are being protected from is our own. As Justice Elena Kagan put it in a searing dissent in 2018:

> Speech is everywhere—a part of every human activity (employment, health care, securities trading, you name it). For that reason, almost all economic and regulatory policy affects or touches speech. So, the majority's road runs long. And at every stop are black-robed rulers overriding citizens' choices. The First Amendment was meant for better things.

And so were we.

CONTRIBUTORS

Samuel Bowles is Arthur Spiegel Research Professor and Director of the Behavioral Sciences Program at Santa Fe Institute.

Ethan Bueno de Mesquita is the Sydney Stein Professor and Deputy Dean at the Harris School of Public Policy at the University of Chicago.

Oren Cass is senior fellow at the Manhattan Institute, and author of *The Once and Future Worker: A Vision for the Renewal of Work in America.*

Joshua Cohen is Editor of *Boston Review*, Professor at Apple University, and Distinguied Senior Fellow of Political Science, Philosophy, and Law at University of California, Berkeley.

Complexity Economists brings an interdisciplinary perspective to economic issues. A list of members is given on the group's forum response.

William Easterly is Professor of Economics at New York University, Codirector of the Development Research Institute, and author of *The White Man's Burden: Why the West's Efforts to Aid the Rest Have Done So Much Ill and So Little Good.*

Alice Evans is a Lecturer in International Development at King's College London and a Research Associate at Harvard University.

Amy Kapczynski is Professor of Law at Yale Law School and cofounder of LPEBlog.org.

Robert Manduca is a doctoral student in Sociology and Social Policy at Harvard University, and a Visiting Scholar at the Center for Spatial Data Science at the University of Chicago.

Suresh Naidu is Associate Professor of Economics and International and Public Affairs at Columbia University.

Caleb Orr is Legislative Assistant for Economic Policy in the Office of Senator Marco Rubio.

Lenore Palladino is Assistant Professor of Economics at University of Massachusetts-Amherst and a Roosevelt Institute Fellow.

Margaret E. Peters is Associate Professor of Political Science at UCLA and author of *Trading Barriers: Immigration and the Remaking of Globalization.*

Corey Robin is Associate Professor of Political Science at Brooklyn College and the CUNY Graduate Center, and the author of *The Reactionary Mind: Conservatism from Edmund Burke to Sarah Palin.*

Dani Rodrik is the Ford Foundation Professor of International Political Economy at Harvard's John F. Kennedy School of Government and currently President-Elect of the International Economic Association. His newest book is *Straight Talk on Trade: Ideas for a Sane World Economy.*

Debra Satz is Marta Sutton Weeks Professor of Ethics in Society and Professor of Philosophy at Stanford University and coauthor of *Economic Analysis, Moral Philosophy and the Public.*

Quinn Slobodian is Associate Professor of History at Wellesley College. His most recent book is *Globalists: The End of Empire and the Birth of Neoliberalism.*

Marshall Steinbaum is Assistant Professor of Economics at the University of Utah and Senior Fellow at the Jain Family Institute.

Arvind Subramanian is Visiting Lecturer at Harvard University and Senior Fellow at the Peterson Institute for International Economics. He is the former Chief Economic Adviser of the Government of India.

Gabriel Zucman is an Assistant Professor of Economics at University of California, Berkeley.